THE READING ADVENTURE

CURATED BY
We Need Diverse Books

ILLUSTRATED BY
Katherine Ahmed, Jake Alexander, Tequitia Andrews,
Ruth Burrows, and Janeen Constantino

CONTENTS

FOREWORD BY ELLEN OH - P. 4

BOLD BEGINNINGS - P. 6

You're never too young for a reading adventure! Featuring simpler stories about friendship, family, and fun, these books are ideal for early and reluctant readers.

BECOMING ME - P. 17

Growing up is exciting, but it can also be scary. Featuring new friendships and changing bodies, the characters in these books are becoming who they are meant to be.

UNEXPECTED JOURNEYS - P. 32

Take a trip without leaving your house. Featuring incredible adventures across land, time, and space, these books will help you see life from a different angle.

MAKE 'EM LAUGH - P. 46

Who doesn't like a good chuckle? From accidentally freezing time to realizing your baby sister is an alien, these books are guaranteed to make you laugh out loud.

ESSENTIAL CONVERSATIONS - P. 56

Life isn't always easy. These stories of disability, discrimination, and displacement will make you think, spark conversations, and maybe even move you to act.

MARVELOUS MYSTERIES - P. 71

Whodunnit, whydunnit, or howdunnit? From missing diamonds to missing family, these books have unexpected twists and turns that will keep you guessing until the very last page.

TIES THAT BIND - P. 82

Familes come in all shapes and sizes. These books feature blended familes, separated families, and multigenerational homes and celebrate family ties of all different kinds.

BOOKS THAT GO BUMP IN THE NIGHT - P. 95

Reader beware—you're in for a scare. Featuring spine-tingling tales of ghosts, graveyards, and haunted houses, these books will have you sleeping with the light on.

STORIES TO SAVE THE DAY - P. 108

Bravery looks different on everyone. From tough princesses to fearless real-life adventurers, these books will inspire you to take chances and follow your dreams, whatever they may be.

BIBLIOGRAPHY - P. 121

WRITING AND READING ACTIVITIES - P. 124

INDEX - P. 126

All the books in this collection have been carefully selected and are suitable for readers between 6 and 12 years old. However, we recommend that a caregiver assesses the suitability of each book before giving it to a child, depending on their individual needs.

FOREWORD

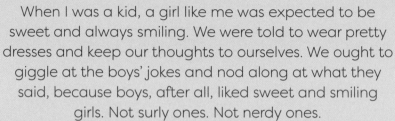

When I was a kid, a girl like me was expected to be sweet and always smiling. We were told to wear pretty dresses and keep our thoughts to ourselves. We ought to giggle at the boys' jokes and nod along at what they said, because boys, after all, liked sweet and smiling girls. Not surly ones. Not nerdy ones.

But I was a nerd. I was surly too and not-so-very sweet. You can imagine how that went over.

I never felt like I quite fit in at school, or most places really, except for one: the library. That's where I'd go to wander through the shelves, running my fingers over the smooth spines. I would gather up a pile of books and leaf through the pages where I'd read about dragons and pirates and faraway kingdoms. I would get lost in the stories, even though I never really saw myself in them.

Until I met Meg Murry.

If you haven't heard of Meg, let me tell you a little bit about her. She's bookish and clumsy and a self-proclaimed oddball. She can also be moody and, according to her principal, "belligerent and uncooperative." In other words, Meg is kind of nerdy and surly—and the brave heroine of Madeleine L'Engle's *A Wrinkle in Time*. I fell in love with her within the first chapter of the book, not in spite of her geekiness or moodiness, but rather because of them. In Meg, I saw me.

In the following pages, you'll find all sorts of Meg Murrys and many other new faces. There's Corinne La Mer, who must save her island home from yellow-eyed tricksters called jumbies. There's also plucky Claudia Kincaid, who decides to run away to the Metropolitan Museum of Art, because her parents just don't appreciate her enough. And I can't forget about Tree-ear, a 12-year-old orphan who dreams about becoming a master potter in medieval Korea.

Here at We Need Diverse Books, we created *The Reading Adventure* to share some of our favorite stories with you. We've compiled 100 books that we think you should check out—some that will make you laugh, some that will make you duck underneath the covers, and some that might make your eyes well up.

So find a comfy reading spot, and thumb through these pages until you find your next book to read. Where will you go?

Sunny Florida perhaps?

A graveyard in Scotland?

Maybe even the far reaches of outer, outer space?

Wherever you choose, my fingers are tightly crossed that you'll find your own Meg Murry very soon.

JO JO MAKOONS: THE USED-TO-BE BEST FRIEND

BY DAWN QUIGLEY

Seven-year-old Jo Jo lives on an Ojibwe reservation with her mother and kokum, and she has a lot on her mind. Like why don't hear and bear rhyme?

Her best cat friend, Mimi, has to get her shots at the dreaded vets, and her best human friend, Fern, seems to be spending a lot of time with new kids at school, leaving Jo Jo behind. When Jo Jo decides to bring Mimi to school in her backpack, there's a bit of a smelly incident in the classroom teepee. But at the end of the day, Jo Jo just wants to stay close to the people—and felines—who matter to her, and she's willing to work to be the best friend that she can be.

QUICK LOOK

This book is about...

☆ Friendship

☆ Indigenous culture

If you like this, check out...

☆ *A Kind of Spark*
  Page 28

☆ *Jada Jones: Rock Star*
  Page 10

AUTHOR INTERVIEW

What inspired you to write this book?

I say that the Jo Jo Makoons series was born from a rejection. I had a picture book rejected in the spring of 2019, and rightly so—it was NOT ready. Then my Native writer friend and mentor, Cynthia Leitich Smith, suggested I try to write a chapter book (this is a type of book where the words tell the story, but there are some pictures too.) I thought, "Well, I can't write a chapter book, because I've never written a chapter book." But then a spunky Ojibwe girl began running around in my mind making me laugh with her antics, and the Jo Jo Makoons book series was born! So Jo Jo is a team effort.

How did you create the main character in this book?

Writing about contemporary Ojibwe kids is really important to me. I want to let all readers, teachers, librarians, and families know that we Natives still exist. I wanted to write a fun, silly book that all readers will enjoy, and the main character just happens to be Ojibwe. I hope children everywhere—especially Native readers—can fall in love with Jo Jo. The world, especially now, is so hard for our young people. I want them to laugh and be able to pause and enjoy the fun world of Jo Jo. I love that Jo Jo sees the world in a slightly unique way and is often the basis for laughs. We all need more laughter in our lives.

Where did you write this book? At home? A coffee shop? A library?

I wrote it sitting at my old kitchen table that is now my writing desk. I love having a window next to me, because I love to daydream as I'm thinking about the story.

ABOUT THE AUTHOR

Dawn Quigley lives with her family in Minnesota. She spends the long winters dreaming about getting out on the lake in a boat. She is a citizen of the Turtle Mountain Band of Chippewa Indians—an Indigenous tribe based in North Dakota.

What was your favorite middle-grade book as a kid?

I'm SO bad at remembering names of books I've read, but I read everything I could get my hands on—backs of cereal boxes, comics...

What's your favorite word?

Send, as in "My book is done—yay. Let's send it to my editor!"

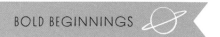
AMBER BROWN IS NOT A CRAYON

BY PAULA DANZIGER

Amber Brown thought that her parents getting a divorce was the toughest thing she'd have to go through. That is until her friend Justin moves away to another state.

Suddenly, Amber and Justin's friendship—which was so easy before—starts to get really, really hard. They used to stand up for each other and stick together in math or spelling no matter what. Now all they do is argue, until a huge fight leads them to stop talking altogether. Amber tries hard to work through all the tough changes that are happening in her life, but will she get her best friend back? This story shows how hard it can be when your world is turned upside down and you don't feel like you can do anything about it.

QUICK LOOK

This book is about...
- ☆ Changing families
- ☆ Changing friendships

If you like this, check out...
- ☆ *Lola Levine Is Not Mean!*   Page 11
- ☆ *Two Naomis*   Pages 82-83

JASMINE TOGUCHI, MOCHI QUEEN
BY DEBBI MICHIKO FLORENCE

Jasmine Toguchi may be only eight, but that doesn't mean she hasn't got what it takes to help with her family's yearly tradition of making mochi.

Every year, Jasmine and her family make a big deal of celebrating New Year's Day. Her Obaachan even flies all the way from Japan to be with them! When it comes to making mochi, there are two rules in the Toguchi house: first, only the men get to pound the rice for the mochi; second, is that kids in Jasmine's family can't help with anything until they are 10 years old. Jasmine is determined to turn these rules upside down and show everyone—including her perfect big sister and bratty older cousin—that she has exactly what it takes to be the best mochi maker!

QUICK LOOK

This book is about...
☆ Family
☆ Japanese culture

If you like this, check out...
☆ *Cilla Lee-Jenkins: Future Author Extraordinaire* Page 13
☆ *Planet Omar: Accidental Trouble Magnet* Page 46

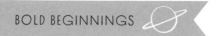

JADA JONES: ROCK STAR
BY KELLY STARLING LYONS

Fourth-grader Jada Jones is excited to start learning about rocks in her class, but she's not so excited that she has to do it without her best friend Mari.

Mari has moved to Phoenix, Arizona, which feels like a million miles from Jada in Raleigh, North Carolina. Jada misses Mari but is hopeful that she will make new friends. When Jada's teacher asks her class to work on a group project about rocks, Jada thinks this just might be her chance to connect with other students and find a new best friend. But Jada's classmate Simone is less interested in the school project and more interested in making sure that Jada doesn't try and steal *her* bestie! Jada might know a lot about science, but she's got a lot to learn about the patience and kindness that's needed to make new friends.

QUICK LOOK

This book is about...

☆ Fitting in
☆ Friendship

If you like this, check out...

☆ *Danny Chung Does Not Do Maths*   Page 86
☆ *Lola Levine Is Not Mean!*   Page 11

LOLA LEVINE IS NOT MEAN!

BY MONICA BROWN

Just because Lola accidentally hurt a classmate during a soccer game doesn't make her a meanie!

Still, that's what everyone calls her at school. Every day that the other kids bully her, Lola finds it harder and harder to see herself for who she really is. Thankfully, Lola's family loves her, and her mom helps Lola use her writing to convince others—including her principal—just how sorry she is about the accident. After a wacky weekend with an escaped guinea pig and some help from her best friend Josh, Lola gets back on the field as a soccer queen instead of the queen of mean.

QUICK LOOK

This book is about...

☆ Girl power
☆ Growing pains

If you like this, check out...

☆ *Jo Jo Makoons: The Used-To-Be Best Friend*   Page 6
☆ *Make Way for Dyamonde Daniel*   Page 12

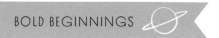

MAKE WAY FOR DYAMONDE DANIEL

BY NIKKI GRIMES

Third-grader Dyamonde Daniel is really, really good at math. She isn't quite so good at adding herself to a group of friends at her new school in Washington Heights, though.

Growing up in Brooklyn, Dyamonde had a family and a best friend. But her parents' divorce broke them all up, and Dyamonde finds herself in a new apartment in Washington Heights with just her mom. At her new school, it doesn't take Dyamonde long to establish herself as a math whiz. But oh, how she would love another best friend! When her new neighbor, Free, joins her classes, Dyamonde decides to see if she + Free might = a great friendship. The trouble is, Free is just so grumpy! Although things start out a little rocky, Dyamonde works with Free and discovers that finding the solution to his problems helps them both.

QUICK LOOK

This book is about...

☆ Moving to a new place
☆ New friendships

If you like this, check out...

☆ *Amber Brown Is Not a Crayon*   Page 8
☆ *Jada Jones: Rock Star* Page 10

CILLA LEE-JENKINS: FUTURE AUTHOR EXTRAORDINAIRE

BY SUSAN TAN

Priscilla "Cilla" Lee-Jenkins has a baby sister on the way, and before she comes, Cilla has got to finish the book she's writing about a really cool person—herself!

Cilla doesn't want her family to forget her when "the Blob" arrives, so she's determined to write down her stories and fulfill her destiny as an author extraordinaire. But she's got other things to worry about, too, like how to connect her white grandparents and her Chinese grandparents despite their cultural differences. Can Cilla bring her family together with her stories and learn to love her new role as big sister?

QUICK LOOK

This book is about...

☆ Family
☆ New siblings

If you like this, check out...

☆ *Jasmine Toguchi, Mochi Queen*   Page 9

☆ *Ways to Make Sunshine* Page 14

13

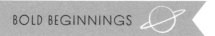

WAYS TO MAKE SUNSHINE

BY RENÉE WATSON

When her father loses his job, fourth-grader Ryan Hart must move to a smaller house in a new neighborhood. Ever the optimist, Ryan refuses to let it get her down.

Ryan has a hard time getting used to the changes in her life, it's true. Things like the disappointing taste of store-brand ice cream and the long wait on the soda can return line. She also feels a little uncomfortable in her best friend's new neighborhood, with its big houses and pools. It seems especially unfriendly to Black girls like Ryan. But even these challenges can't dent Ryan's natural optimism for long. She's determined to make sunshine wherever she goes, and as she does so, both Ryan and her family grow under its brightness and warmth.

QUICK LOOK

This book is about...
- ☆ Family
- ☆ Growing pains

If you like this, check out...
- ☆ *Little Robot*
  Page 44
- ☆ *The Doughnut Fix*
  Page 55

JUPITER STORM
BY MARTI DUMAS

Twelve-year-old Jacquelyn Marie is not the oldest of her parents' six children, but she is the one in charge!

It's usually Jackie who runs the show and keeps everyone and everything on track. Then one day, she finds a peculiar chrysalegg growing on one of her snapdragon plants, and it becomes all she can think and care about. But when a dragon hatches from the chrysalegg one night, Jackie needs to quickly figure out how to keep a flying, fire-breathing lizard a secret from her very big—and very close—family!

QUICK LOOK

This book is about...

☆ Family
☆ Magical adventures

If you like this, check out...

☆ *Dragons in a Bag*
   Page 35
☆ *Lola Levine Is Not Mean!*   Page 11

ONE CRAZY SUMMER

BY RITA WILLIAMS-GARCIA

Delphine is in charge of her younger sisters Vonetta and Fern, and what she says goes— at least in the beginning.

The three sisters travel from New York to California to meet their mother, Cecile, who left them to be raised by their daddy and grandmother. While Cecile—aka Sister Nzila—isn't the mom they expect, Oakland provides more excitement in one summer than the girls imagine they will ever have in Brooklyn. Cecile is a member of the Black Panther Party, and as Delphine, Vonetta, and Fern take classes and find friends at the center where the Black Panthers serve the community, they learn a lot more about who they are and who they have the power to be.

QUICK LOOK

This book is about...

☆ Black history
☆ Family

If you like this, check out...

☆ *A Good Kind of Trouble*   Page 62
☆ *The Samosa Rebellion* Page 110

ROLLING WARRIOR

BY JUDITH HEUMANN AND KRISTEN JOINER

Contracting polio as a little girl didn't stop Judith Heumann. And when schools, jobs, and laws tried to stop her, she fought back.

This is the true story of Judith Heumann and her decades of fighting for her own humanity and the humanity of other disabled people. After being excluded from mainstream education, Judith began campaigning for the rights of disabled people. Since then, she has led sit-ins and protests and worked to get disabled people the help and support they need. It's not always easy to do the right thing, but Judith Heumann knows it's important. Read all about her life, courage, and determination.

QUICK LOOK

This book is about...

☆ Activism
☆ Disability

If you like this, check out...

☆ *A Good Kind of Trouble*   Page 62
☆ *Wink*   Page 58

MERCI SUÁREZ CHANGES GEARS

BY MEG MEDINA

It's Merci Suárez's first year in middle school, but sixth grade is NOT off to a great start.

Merci doesn't exactly feel like she fits in at Seaward Pines, the private school her and her brother have a scholarship to. Merci has to balance her academic responsibilities, changing classrooms and teachers, work, AND her jealous classmate Edna Santos. On top of all of that, Merci's Lolo is growing more and more forgetful. When Merci finally learns the truth about her grandfather, she must switch gears again to deal with her biggest challenge yet.

QUICK LOOK

This book is about...

☆ Family life
☆ Struggling to fit in

If you like this, check out...

☆ *Free Lunch*
Page 67
☆ *New Kid*
Page 56

AUTHOR INTERVIEW

How did you create the main character in this book?

I was inspired to write the Merci Suárez trilogy when I was invited to write a short story featuring a Latinx protagonist for the anthology *Flying Lessons and Other Stories*. She's a mixture of self-doubt, self-realization, and sarcasm, which feels exactly right against the backdrop of middle school. Also, it was such a pleasure to draw her as part of a realistic Latinx family that readers found relatable.

What tips do you have for young writers?

Read widely. You'll not only be adding words to your vocabulary, but you'll also be adding writing strategies to your toolbox. When you start developing your own work, you'll be recalling your reading and using some of the same strategies even as you add your own style and voice.

What was the process like in getting this book published?

Writing a book requires your artistic side, but publishing a book requires having some business sense about the publishing industry. It helps to understand who the players are in the industry and how all the parts work together.

How do you keep going when you get stuck/writing gets hard?

I remind myself that I will find the solution eventually. Dry periods are always part of the process, just as revision is part of the process. While I'm frozen, I take a little time away and work on something else. I ask friends for input and advice. I make sure I'm getting some exercise. Somehow, those things always point to the answer in the end.

ABOUT THE AUTHOR

Meg Medina is a Cuban American author. She grew up in Queens, New York, but now lives in Richmond, Virginia, with her family. She speaks Spanish fluently, and she works on community projects in her spare time.

What's your favorite word?

My favorite word is abundance. I like the round sound of the "b" and the long "s" sound at the end. But more than anything, I like that it suggests generosity and the idea of giving and enjoying more than the bare minimum. Just think of all the ways we can practice abundance in the world!

THE MOON WITHIN

BY AIDA SALAZAR

Celi lives in Oakland, California. She dreams of being a herbalist and loves to dance. But now that she is almost 12, her world is beginning to change.

Celi is proud of the community she shares with her Afro-Puerto Rican father, Mexican mother, and little brother. But there's something she doesn't feel so comfortable about: the upcoming traditional moon ceremony to celebrate her first period. Celi thinks she has a right to make her own choices, but getting her mom to understand that is a struggle. Celi is dealing with the ways her body is changing and at the same time supporting her best friend through another important transition. Through a series of short poems, this book shows the many ways Celi's care, support, and love bloom as bold and bright as a new moon.

QUICK LOOK

This book is about...

☆ LGBTQ+
☆ Growing up

If you like this, check out...

☆ *Melissa (George)*
  Page 30
☆ *So Done*
  Page 94

STARFISH

BY LISA FIPPS

Hurt by the people who make fun of her weight—including her mother—Ellie Montgomery-Hofstein is happiest in her swimming pool.

There, she can float and spread out as wide as she wants to. There, she doesn't have to worry about the Fat Girl Rules that she follows to cope with the cruel behavior and comments from those around her. Ellie is finding it tough to find love and acceptance in a world that is determined to put her down because of her weight. But her story proves that being happy and being thin don't always go hand in hand. Quick chapters written in verse make this a fast, fun read.

QUICK LOOK

This book is about...

☆ Accepting yourself

☆ Family

If you like this, check out...

☆ *Free Lunch*
Page 67

☆ *Hello, Universe*
Pages 88-89

AMERICAN AS PANEER PIE

BY SUPRIYA KELKAR

Lekha is living a double life in her tiny town.

In one life, she can celebrate all the wonderful things about her Indian culture and community. In the other life, as the only Indian American girl in her small town, she has to hide her heritage so that the kids at her school don't tease her. When another Indian girl, Avantika, moves into town, Lekha is surprised to learn that Avantika isn't afraid of anyone, or of being herself. And Avantika DEFINITELY isn't afraid to stand up to anyone who disrespects her. Watching Avantika, Lekha starts to wonder whether maybe it's time to stop being afraid and let the world see every part of her.

QUICK LOOK

This book is about...

☆ Being yourself
☆ Indian culture

If you like this, check out...

☆ *Pie in the Sky*
   Pages 50-51
☆ *The Insiders*
   Pages 26-27

AMINA'S VOICE

BY HENA KHAN

Despite having an amazing voice, sixth-grader Amina Khokar's stage fright stops her from singing in public.

Amina's best friend Soojin wants Amina to share her talent with the world, but Amina's visiting uncle disapproves of her love for music. Soon, Soojin is talking about changing her name and hanging out with a different crowd, leaving Amina unsure whether she fits in with her friend anymore. When Amina's Islamic Center is viciously attacked, Amina's music could be the signal to everyone that change and acceptance are necessary for their entire community—if only she can get up the courage to perform.

QUICK LOOK

This book is about...

☆ Finding courage
☆ Racism

If you like this, check out...

☆ *American as Paneer Pie*   Page 22
☆ *The Magic in Changing Your Stars*   Page 32

OUT OF WONDER

BY KWAME ALEXANDER WITH CHRIS COLDERLEY AND MARJORY WENTWORTH

Poems have always held a special power over Kwame Alexander. In this book, he celebrates, champions, and shares the wonders of poetry.

Kwame's introduction to the world of poetry shows how poems can lift our hearts, open our eyes, and delight our spirits, whatever their style. It's all about the beauty of simple words. This collection of 20 poets Kwame loves includes Lucille Clifton, e.e. cummings, Nikki Giovanni, and Robert Frost. There are easy rhymes, there are haikus, there are poems in funky shapes with jazzy rhythms, and they're all paired with illustrations that make words and pictures move together like music and dance. Every poet-in-the-making will find something to inspire them here.

QUICK LOOK

This book is about...

☆ Poetry

☆ The joy of reading

If you like this, check out...

☆ Brown Girl Dreaming Page 84

☆ The 1619 Project: Born on the Water   Page 68

BLENDED

BY SHARON M. DRAPER

After their divorce, it's hard for 11-year-old Isabella's parents to not get mad at each other for Every. Little. Thing.

Isabella already has enough to worry about with a big piano recital coming up and the pressure of trying to find her place at school. But when someone puts a noose in her friend Imani's locker, it's not just Isabella who's worried. Everything is a big, messy mix, and Isabella struggles to deal with her parents remarrying new people and the racial prejudice she faces everywhere from school to at the mall, and even at home. Will Isabella get the smooth blended life she desperately wants?

QUICK LOOK

This book is about...

☆ Changing families

☆ Racism

If you like this, check out...

☆ *Front Desk*
Page 34

☆ *Two Naomis*
Pages 82-83

THE INSIDERS

BY MARK OSHIRO

Héctor Muñoz never had to hide how awesome he is when he lived in San Francisco.

But things are different in Orangeville. When he starts getting bullied at his new school because he's gay, Héctor is not sure what to do except run. One day, he discovers a magical janitor's closet that gives him what he needs exactly when he needs it. A bed when he can't sleep? No problem! Cereal when he's hungry? You got it! Then one day, the closet gives him two friends from totally different parts of the country! Together, they help Héctor turn things around at school, and with some help from his amazing abuela, Héctor gets back to being his fabulous self.

QUICK LOOK

This book is about...

☆ Making new friends
☆ Magical adventures

If you like this, check out...

☆ *Melissa (George)*
   Page 30

☆ *Sal & Gabi Break the Universe*   Page 38

AUTHOR INTERVIEW

What inspired you to write this book?

It's actually a sad story. I was viciously bullied in middle school, and when I finally got the courage to tell an adult—in my case, the school counselor—they blamed the bullying on me, because they said I made myself an easy target by acting gay. It was the first striking moment I can recall thinking, "Oh, I can't trust adults." There is a plot line in *The Insiders* that follows something similar, but I took it to a fantastical place as an exploration of what I had wished had happened.

How did you create the main character in this book?

There's a tiny bit of myself in Héctor. I didn't discover theater until my junior year of high school, but that, combined with an English teacher who coached me through public speaking, allowed me to come out of my shell. So I wanted to start with a character who was already past that, who was already out, and who was already sure of who he was.

Where did you write this book? At home? A coffee shop? The library?

The first draft of this book was started on January 4, 2020, while I was on a writing retreat with my friends. We were in Hawaii! The bulk of it was written between two apartments in New York and a hotel in Miami that I escaped to when I couldn't deal with NYC's cold weather. It was written in 62 days.

How do you keep going when you get stuck/writing gets hard?

I actually stop! The goal is to reset my brain. More often than not, I figure out what was keeping me stuck, and it's usually because I made a decision earlier on that messed things up.

ABOUT THE AUTHOR

Mark Oshiro lives in Atlanta, Georgia. When they're not writing, they're trying to pet as many dogs as possible.

What was your favorite book as a kid?

My favorites alternated between whatever new Beverly Cleary book I found in the library and whatever new *Goosebumps* book came out. Also, *The Lion, The Witch, and the Wardrobe* had an immense influence on me. It's where the idea of magical closets came from in the first place.

What's your favorite word?

Punctuated.

27

A KIND OF SPARK
BY ELLE MCNICOLL

Everyone in Addie's small Scottish town wants to forget that the witch trials ever happened. But Addie doesn't.

When she learns about the witch trials that took the lives of women in her town, Addie decides to build a memorial to those women. Addie knows what it's like to be different—she has to put up with the kids at school who make fun of her because she's autistic—and she's determined that the witches should be remembered. Addie believes in her memorial, and she's prepared to fight for it. And along the way, she starts to believe in herself, too.

QUICK LOOK

This book is about...

⭐ Historical events
⭐ Being different

If you like this, check out...

⭐ *Hurricane Child*
  Page 90
⭐ *Just South of Home*
  Page 97

THE FIRST RULE OF PUNK

BY CELIA C. PÉREZ

Twelve-year-old Malú has just moved in with her mom in Chicago, and she's ready to rock at her new school!

The only thing is, Posada Middle School isn't exactly punk rock friendly. Being at Posada has Malú thinking a lot about who she is and who she wants to be. She may not be the perfect Mexican student and hija like her classmate Selena, but she's still cool, right? Malú's dad reminds her that the first rule of punk is to be yourself. So Malú starts her own band and sets out to change the hearts and minds of the grown-ups around her.

QUICK LOOK

This book is about...

☆ Being yourself

☆ Moving somewhere new

If you like this, check out...

☆ *Merci Suárez Changes Gears*   Page 38

☆ *Wink* Page 58

MELISSA (GEORGE)
BY ALEX GINO

Ten-year-old George knows that she's a girl. Period. She just needs to figure out how to tell everyone else around her.

No more hiding her love of fashion magazines in her closet. No more having to pretend she's okay with everyone thinking she's a boy. George is ready to be who she is, not just in secret, but with all the people she loves. With the help of her best friend Kelly, George hatches a plan to use the class play—*Charlotte's Web*—as her big opportunity to share with her friends and family exactly who she really is.

QUICK LOOK

This book is about...

☆ LGBTQ+

☆ Being yourself

If you like this, check out...

☆ *Inside Out & Back Again*   Page 40

☆ *Me, My Dad and the End of the Rainbow*   Page 91

AUTHOR INTERVIEW

What inspired you to write this book?

Not having read books like it when I was a kid. *Melissa* isn't autobiographical, but I think if I had access to good transgender representation earlier, I would have had an easier road in understanding and accepting myself. I want to provide that for kids now.

How did you create the main character in this book?

The first image I had for Melissa takes place at the end of the book, which—not to spoil too much—involved a young trans girl being herself in public for the first time with her best friend. From there, it became a question of how to develop a story that would show how special that simple moment was.

Where did you write this book? At home? A coffee shop? The library?

Home home home home home. Some people like to listen to music when they write. I am not one of those people. Not only do I prefer to write with no one else in the room, I prefer to write with no one else in the house. My brain goes pretty deep when I'm creating, and when I get interrupted, I can get startled.

What was the process like in getting this book published?

The hardest part of *Melissa*, by far, was writing it. It took me about 12 years, and when I started in 2003, it was a pretty far-fetched idea to think that a traditional publisher would ever take on a middle-grade book with a transgender main character. By the time I had an agent and a submission-ready manuscript, it was 2014, and publishers were eager for trans stories.

GEORGE

ABOUT THE AUTHOR

Alex Gino has written five books, including *Melissa*. They love glitter, ice cream, and gardening. They once spent 18 months in an RV traveling through 44 US states, but they're now settled in the Hudson Valley, New York with two mischievous black cats: Thunderbolt and Lightning.

What was your favorite middle-grade book as a kid?

One of my favorite books was *Where The Sidewalk Ends* by Shel Silverstein. Silverstein's poetry showed me that you could be silly and meaningful at the same time, and that it is very hard, but perhaps not impossible, to write a poem on the neck of a running giraffe.

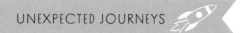
THE MAGIC IN CHANGING YOUR STARS

BY LEAH HENDERSON

When 11-year-old Ailey Benjamin Lane's nerves get the better of him, he ends up losing the big part he wanted in the school musical.

Gramps tells Ailey the story of how, when he was young, he also messed up a big opportunity to perform. When Ailey steps into his grandfather's shoes, he is transported back in time to 1930s Harlem, where he meets legendary Black figures. Even though he's not sure how he'll get back home to his own time, Ailey does all he can to help the young version of his grandfather chase his dreams and change the alignment of his stars.

QUICK LOOK

This book is about...
☆ Family
☆ Magical adventures

If you like this, check out...
☆ *Dragons in a Bag*   Page 35
☆ *Just South of Home*   Page 97

LILY & KOSMO IN OUTER OUTER SPACE

BY JONATHAN ASHLEY

Lily's parents are mean. They hate her favorite radio show and the new haircut she's given herself. So she grabs her little brother, Alfie, and heads for Outer Outer Space with Spacetronaut Kosmo.

When Kosmo crashes into Lily's life, she can't wait to run away with him. But she soon finds out he isn't perfect. Kosmo and his all-boy crew constantly underestimate girls! Fortunately, Lily turns out to be an amazing adventurer, outsmarting the bad guys and impressing her new friends. Kosmo and the other Spacetronauts bring silliness and adventure, while Lily gets to be a real space hero like the ones she loves on the radio. Eventually, it's time to come back down to Earth, but can Lily get two-year-old Alfie home before her parents notice? One thing's for sure—this won't be the last time Lily explores the Murky Way!

QUICK LOOK

This book is about...

⭐ Adventures in other dimensions
⭐ Girl power

If you like this, check out...

⭐ *From the Mixed-Up Files of Mrs. Basil E. Frankweiler*   Page 72
⭐ *The A-Z Djinn Detective Agency*   Page 76

FRONT DESK

BY KELLY YANG

Money is always tight for Mia Tang and her parents, but they are happy to be part of the tight-knit community at the motel where they work.

As recent immigrants from China, the Tang family know how hard it can be to adjust to a new place. Despite the risks, they do their best to help other immigrants out—even though it means they could lose their jobs and face the anger of Mr. Yao, the motel's mean manager. When one of the Tang's neighbors is accused of stealing a car, Mia shows up for him in a big way and helps clear his name and, in the process, exposes the harmful impact of racism and the power of community.

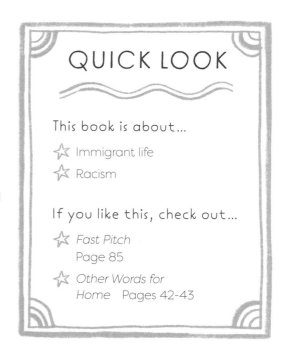

QUICK LOOK

This book is about...
- ☆ Immigrant life
- ☆ Racism

If you like this, check out...
- ☆ *Fast Pitch*
  Page 85
- ☆ *Other Words for Home*   Pages 42-43

DRAGONS IN A BAG

BY ZETTA ELLIOTT

Jaxson's plans for the day don't involve helping Ma, a witch, deliver dragons to a mystical realm. But when you jump into a magical transporter, amazing things can happen!

Nine-year-old Jax isn't short of determination. He's willing to cross dimensions, go back in time to outrun dinosaurs, and even stand up to his mom—all to show that he's got what it takes to be a witch's apprentice. But will he go and spoil it by failing in the most important task of all—not letting the dragons out of the bag? This sweet story begins and ends in Brooklyn where there's still a little bit of magic, a lot of mischief, and some mysteries that Jax and his friends help to solve.

QUICK LOOK

This book is about...

☆ Adventures in other dimensions

☆ Friendship

If you like this, check out...

☆ *Ghost Squad*
Page 99

☆ *The Serpent's Secret*
Pages 112-113

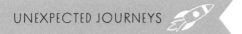

A SINGLE SHARD

BY LINDA SUE PARK

Young Tree-ear lives a simple life under a bridge with his friend Crane-man. But before long, a costly mistake puts him on a new, winding path.

Tree-ear is fascinated by the work of local potters. He'd love to learn the skill, but how? In his land, a potter's skills are usually passed down from father to son, and Tree-ear is an orphan. Things look bad for Tree-ear when he accidentally breaks a box crafted by potter Min, but the need to pay for the breakage might just be his big opportunity to learn the craft from a true master. With this dream in his heart, Tree-ear prepares to travel long distances from the only home he knows in order to impress Min and show the world his loyalty and determination.

QUICK LOOK

This book is about...

☆ Epic adventures
☆ Korean culture and history

If you like this, check out...

☆ *Roll of Thunder, Hear My Cry*   Page 87
☆ *The Boy Who Harnessed the Wind*   116

AUTHOR INTERVIEW

What inspired you to write this book?

My parents are immigrants from Korea. I wanted to learn more about the history of the land that my family came from. I learned that during the 11th and 12th centuries, Koreans made the most beautiful and valuable pottery in the world. That made me feel proud about being Korean, and I wrote *A Single Shard* so I could share what I learned. Everyone's family, community, and culture has stories that need to be shared. It's how we connect with one another.

What tips do you have for young writers?

FAIL UP. That means make mistakes, learn from them, and do a little better the next time. Along with most of the good writers I know, I really and truly LOVE the revision process; figuring out how I can make the story better. Every draft I write—for *A Single Shard*, I wrote eight drafts, but my record is for a book called *When My Name Was Keoko* (37 drafts!)—is a chance for me to fail up!

How do you keep going when you get stuck/writing gets hard?

Two things to help me get unstuck: (1) tiny tasks. I give myself very small assignments like: "Today I just have to write ONE paragraph," or even one sentence. Often, that gets me started, and I end up writing more. (2) PERMISSION TO WRITE TERRIBLY! So the assignment is actually: "Today I just have to write two VERY BAD sentences." I don't put any pressure on myself to write something *good,* because I know I'm going to revise it many times.

ABOUT THE AUTHOR

Linda Sue Park is a Korean American writer. She has traveled to 49 states and more than 30 countries. She enjoys knitting, baseball, and snorkeling, and her favorite library is in Dublin, Ireland.

What was your favorite middle-grade book as a kid?

Too many favorites to list! A few books I reread dozens of times: *Roosevelt Grady* by Louisa Shotwell; *The Saturdays* (and the rest of the *Melendy* series) by Elizabeth Enright; and *Tales of a Korean Grandmother* by Francis Carpenter.

What's your favorite word?

Artichoke.

SAL & GABI BREAK THE UNIVERSE

BY CARLOS HERNANDEZ

As soon as amateur magician Sal moves to Miami, he's in trouble. Apparently, opening wormholes to the multiverse is frowned upon. Only one person seems sympathetic—his new best friend Gabi.

Gabi is the student council president and a natural problem-solver. So figuring out how to stop Sal's blood sugar problems from breaking the universe is just the challenge she's looking for. It turns out the mystery lies with the "calamitrons" Sal releases when he relaxes and thinks of his late mother, Mami Muerta. Learning about "calamity physics" together marks the beginning of a supercharged friendship between Sal and Gabi—one that's filled with hilarious hijinks and sticky situations.

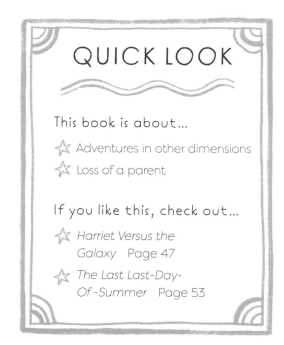

QUICK LOOK

This book is about...

☆ Adventures in other dimensions

☆ Loss of a parent

If you like this, check out...

☆ *Harriet Versus the Galaxy*   Page 47

☆ *The Last Last-Day-Of-Summer*   Page 53

DEAR SWEET PEA

BY JULIE MURPHY

Sweet Pea doesn't need two rooms OR two houses. She doesn't need her parents divorcing, and she DEFINITELY doesn't need to feel bad for her ex-best friend who is now her biggest bully at school.

Unfortunately, Sweet Pea can't stop any of those things from happening. But when the town's advice columnist, Miss. Flora Mae, leaves Sweet Pea in charge of delivering her mail, Sweet Pea can't seem to stop sneaking her own answers into the column. When her secret meddling is revealed, Sweet Pea must pick up the pieces of her friendships and come clean to everyone—including herself—about how she really feels about all the changes that are happening in her life.

QUICK LOOK

This book is about...

⭐ Friendship

⭐ Growing pains

If you like this, check out...

⭐ *Stand Up, Yumi Chung!* Page 49

⭐ *Starfish* Page 21

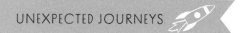
INSIDE OUT & BACK AGAIN

BY THANHHA LAI

Hà is 10 when the Vietnam War erupts, and she is forced to leave her homeland for Alabama.

In her new town, Hà faces terrifying hatred and racism. It's at home with her new neighbors, and it's at school where she is called names, tripped, and even followed home while bullies tease her. Thankfully, Hà has her family to support her, especially her brothers who—despite dealing with their own struggles in the US—still take time to connect with their sister. Written in verse, this book beautifully shares the story of a little girl's resilience and strength in the face of the loss of her father and her home.

QUICK LOOK

This book is about...

☆ Displacement

☆ Losing a parent

If you like this, check out...

☆ *Other Words for Home*   Pages 42-43

☆ *Pie in the Sky* Pages 50-51

NEVER CAUGHT, THE STORY OF ONA JUDGE

BY ERICA ARMSTRONG DUNBAR & KATHLEEN VAN CLEVE

This is the incredible story of Ona Judge. Enslaved by US president George Washington and his wife, Martha, Ona ran away from them and the brutality of slavery.

Even though Ona Judge was born into slavery, she refused to remain enslaved. Newspapers called for her to be brought back after she ran away, and even though she was hunted for years after she left the Washingtons, Ona never stopped fighting to stay free. Her journey took her across the northeastern United States but never back to her family in the south and never back into the grip of slavery. This is the inspiring true story of a woman who was never caught and died proud and free.

QUICK LOOK

This book is about...

☆ Black history

☆ Slavery

If you like this, check out...

☆ *The 1619 Project: Born on the Water*   Page 68

☆ *The Boy Who Harnessed the Wind*   Page 116

OTHER WORDS FOR HOME

BY JASMINE WARGA

Jude doesn't want to leave her home in Syria, but when violence in her hometown threatens the safety of her and her pregnant mother, they move to the US.

Her new life in Cincinnati, Ohio is unlike anything Jude could ever have imagined. As a Muslim immigrant, she faces prejudice from the locals—who don't believe that she belongs—while also adjusting to being in a new, loud place without her father and brother. Jude eventually begins to bond with her uncle and his family and finds community in her English class. Written in short, beautiful verse, this is a quick and thoughtful read.

QUICK LOOK

This book is about...

☆ Culture clashes

☆ Immigration

If you like this, check out...

☆ *Front Desk*
Page 34

☆ *The Night Diary*
Page 61

AUTHOR INTERVIEW

How did you create the main character in this book?

Jude is loosely based on my own cousin whose name is also Jude. My cousin Jude—like Jude from the book—loves American movies and has the world's biggest heart.

Where did you write this book? At home? A coffee shop? The library?

In my writing study on the third floor of my old house, which was located in Cincinnati in the neighborhood of Clifton, where the book takes place. Then my family moved to Chicago, and I heavily revised bits of the book in various coffee shops throughout the city.

What tips do you have for young writers?

Read! Read diversely and widely—read everything you can get your hands on. And also write. Write as much as you can. Think of your writing skills like a muscle—they will get stronger the more you use them.

ABOUT THE AUTHOR

Jasmine Warga is a Jordanian American author. She grew up in Ohio but now lives in Chicago with her husband, two daughters, a cat, and a dog. Her favorite ice cream is Graeter's black raspberry chip.

What's your favorite word?

Serendipity.

What was your favorite middle-grade book as a kid?

The Bridge to Terabithia.

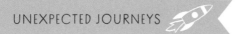

LITTLE ROBOT

BY BEN HATKE

When a lonely five-year-old girl finds a lost robot, the two end up sharing a (mostly) happy new friendship.

The child is so excited to finally have someone to play with, and even though the robot imagines that there might be more out there for it, the child is more than happy for it to be just the two of them always. Little does she know that other robots—and one in particular with a gift for repairing robots—are actually the key to keeping their friendship safe forever. Most of this story is wordless with some chirps and beeps from the robot, but the pictures show the bond that grows between the pair.

QUICK LOOK

This book is about...

★ Fitting in

★ Friendship

If you like this, check out...

★ *Lola Levine Is Not Mean!*
  Page 11

★ *Prime Baby*
  Page 52

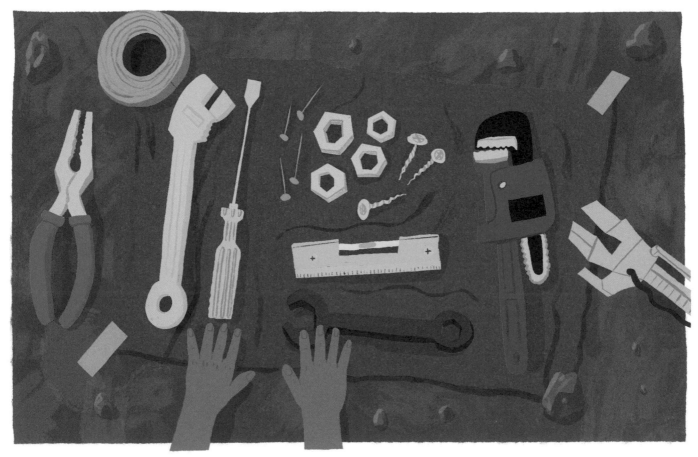

SISTERS OF THE NEVERSEA

BY CYNTHIA LEITICH SMITH

Lily and her stepsister Wendy are best friends, and they're worried about what will happen if their blended family splits.

The two 12-year-olds live in Tulsa, Oklahoma with Wendy's Muscogee Creek mother and Wendy's English father. One night, before they're set to spend the summer apart, Peter Pan shows up and asks Wendy to travel with him to Neverland. But it soon becomes clear that Peter's not the kind-hearted, forever young boy they thought he was, and it's up to Lily and Wendy to get them and their little brother home safe and sound.

QUICK LOOK

This book is about...

☆ Family

☆ Magical adventures

If you like this, check out...

☆ *Two Naomis*
Pages 82-83

✷ *Zombierella: Fairy Tales Gone Bad*   Page 98

PLANET OMAR: ACCIDENTAL TROUBLE MAGNET

BY ZANIB MIAN

Omar has just moved to a new house, and that means a new school, new neighbors, and—hopefully—new friends.

Omar's imagination can often run a little wild, but his reality is also pretty action filled. First of all, he needs to learn to handle his mean neighbor Mrs. Rogers, who constantly complains about Omar's family and calls them "The Muslims." Then there's Daniel, the kid at school who has a problem with Omar's skin color and religion. All this is happening during Ramadan, and Omar's going to have to stay out of trouble—accidental or not—if he wants to make it to Eid and the promise of yummy food and presents!

QUICK LOOK

This book is about...

☆ Moving to a new place
☆ Muslim culture

If you like this, check out...

☆ *Jo Jo Makoons: The Used-To-Be Best Friend* Page 6

☆ *My Laugh-Out-Loud Life: Mayhem Mission* Page 48

HARRIET VERSUS THE GALAXY

BY SAMANTHA BAINES

Harriet thinks her hearing aid is just the regular kind. That is until she realizes that it allows her to understand aliens all the way across the galaxy!

Ten-year-old Harriet has no idea that her gran is a secret agent who works for an intergalactic organization that defends earth from alien invasions. But when Harriet finds an alien under her bed, she teams up with her gran and next-door neighbor Robin, and with the help of her hearing aid, they're ready to defend earth against another attack. It seems that there's going to be more to living with her gran than just drinking tea and knitting socks!

QUICK LOOK

This book is about...

☆ Family secrets

☆ Intergalactic adventures

If you like this, check out...

☆ *El Deafo*
Page 120

☆ *Ghost Squad*
Page 99

MY LAUGH-OUT-LOUD LIFE: MAYHEM MISSION
BY BURHANA ISLAM

Yousuf Ali Khan is not ready to be the man of the house yet. But that's exactly what's about to happen!

Yousef's older sister has always been the responsible one. But when Yousuf realizes that he's going to have to step up when she gets married and goes to start her new life with her husband, he hatches a plan to stop the wedding. With his cousin Aadam as his partner in crime, Yusuf will stop at nothing to make sure that his mission creates as much mayhem as possible—even if it means he has to face his Amma and Nanu head on!

QUICK LOOK

This book is about...

☆ Indian culture
☆ Family

If you like this, check out...

☆ *Agent Zaiba Investigates: The Missing Diamonds* Page 78

☆ *Anisha, Accidental Detective* Page 77

STAND UP, YUMI CHUNG!

BY JESSICA KIM

Yumi Chung can definitely take a joke, and she's pretty great at dishing them out, too!

If only she had the chance to perform her stand-up, people would see her and immediately know she's a star. There's no time right now, though, because Yumi's life is less about stand-up and more about studying so she can get a scholarship to private school. But when Yumi is mistaken for someone else, she winds up in a youth comedy camp with her favorite comedian. Yumi starts to lead a double life, hoping that she doesn't get into trouble for pretending to be someone else, and REALLY hoping that her parents get to see just how good she is onstage.

QUICK LOOK

This book is about...

☆ Following your dreams
☆ Mistaken identity

If you like this, check out...

☆ *Amina's Voice*
Page 23

☆ *Dear Sweet Pea*
Page 39

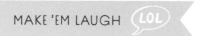
PIE IN THE SKY

BY REMY LAI

The only thing Jingwen is enjoying right now are his dreams about baking.

He's just moved to Australia with his mother and little brother, Yanghao, and he HATES it. School sucks because he doesn't speak English, and to make things worse, Yanghao is learning the language very quickly. Jingwen decides to go from dreaming about baking to actually baking, even though he's forbidden to use the oven when he's home alone. Jingwen decides to start working his way through the list of 12 cakes his dad created before he died, and that means hiding his and his brother's kitchen hijinks from his mom! There's a lot that can go wrong baking under that kind of pressure, but it's worth it for Jingwen to keep his dad's dream alive.

QUICK LOOK

This book is about...

☆ Immigrant experiences

☆ Losing a parent

If you like this, check out...

☆ *Other Words for Home*
   Pages 42-43

☆ *The Doughnut Fix*
   Page 55

AUTHOR INTERVIEW

What inspired you to write this book?

I was inspired by my own childhood. At nine years old, I immigrated and had to learn English. I remember how hard it was initially, trying to make new friends when you couldn't communicate.

How did you create the main character in this book?

Jingwen first appeared to me with his brother, Yanghao, and they were secretly baking. I had a rough idea about what their personalities would be, and I had a lot of fun refining their characters to allow them to bounce off each other and for them to bring out the worst—and the best—in each other.

Where did you write this book? At home? A coffee shop? The library?

I like to do a lot of writing in my head, so most of it was done while I was walking my dogs. Other than that, it was mostly at home and a friend's beautiful house that I happened to be house-sitting.

What tips do you have for young writers?

Remember to have fun, especially if you're a writer with publication goals.

What was the process like in getting this book published?

It was exhilarating. I had written many stories that received so many rejections, and *Pie in the Sky* finally got me my agent and my first book deal.

ABOUT THE AUTHOR

Remy Lai lives in Brisbane, Australia. She loves to explore the woods around her home with her two dogs—Poop-Roller and Bossy Boots—by her side.

What was your favorite middle-grade book as a kid?

As a kid, I actually read many adult books, but for middle grade, it would have to be the *Fear Street* series. I devoured spooky stories.

What's a middle-grade book that you wish you had written and why?

I wish I had written the *Dog Man* series. They capture not only all the joy and fun of being a kid but also the joy and fun the adult is having writing and drawing the books.

PRIME BABY

BY GENE LUEN YANG

Eight-year-old Thaddeus is a perfectly happy only child—that is, until his baby sister, Maddie, comes along. And Maddie is ~~probably~~ definitely an alien.

Maddie only says "ga" in patterns of prime numbers, so Thaddeus does the sensible thing and prepares himself for the alien invasion he's sure she's bringing. However, he can't quite believe it when the aliens *do* come—as it turns out Maddie is a gateway for them get to Earth! Thaddeus isn't a big fan of the aliens' plans to help make the world a better place for everyone. But he starts to realize that being bossy and mean all the time can make you lonely, and perhaps little sisters aren't so bad after all.

QUICK LOOK

This book is about...

☆ A new sibling
☆ Intergalactic adventures

If you like this, check out...

☆ *Cilla Lee-Jenkins: Future Author Extraordinaire* Page 13
☆ *Harriet Versus the Galaxy* Page 47

THE LAST LAST-DAY-OF-SUMMER

BY LAMAR GILES

Middle-schoolers Otto and Sheed are legendary adventurers. There isn't much these clever cousins cannot handle. Except, perhaps, time itself...

Another fun summer is coming to an end, and the dynamic duo are desperate to make the most of the precious time they have left. When the creepy and mysterious Mr. Flux gives them a magical camera, he doesn't tell them one important thing about it: The camera actually freezes time. With their whole town now frozen in place—and clearly unhappy about it—Otto and Sheed must stop Mr. Flux's plans for revenge. Luckily, they are joined by some unexpected allies, including Father Time himself!

QUICK LOOK

This book is about...

☆ Magical adventures

☆ Solving mysteries

If you like this, check out...

☆ *Holes*
  Page 71

☆ *The Season of Styx Malone*   Page 80

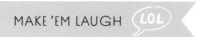

SAM WU IS NOT AFRAID OF GHOSTS

BY KATIE AND KEVIN TSANG

Sam Wu is actually afraid of a lot of things... including the ghosts in his favorite TV show *Space Blasters*. He just doesn't want anyone to know!

When Sam wets himself on a class trip, he's given a nickname he can't shake: Scaredy-Cat Sam. Sam's two best friends try to make him feel better, but that just gives him something else to be afraid of. He's afraid that if he invites them over to his home, they might think his Chinese family's food and language are not "normal!" With the help of his friends and his not-so-bad-after-all little sister, Sam is determined to prove that he's not a scaredy-cat. But his quest for courage becomes less about conquering bullies—or evil ninja felines—and more about overcoming his own self-doubt. It's a ghost story that isn't—in the end—quite a ghost story.

QUICK LOOK

This book is about...

☆ Being brave
☆ Family

If you like this, check out...

☆ *Lily & Kosmo in Outer Outer Space*   Page 33
☆ *Planet Omar: Accidental Trouble Magnet*   Page 46

THE DOUGHNUT FIX

BY JESSIE JANOWITZ

When 12-year-old Tristan moves from New York City to the teeny-tiny town of Petersville, he's not sure how he's going to survive.

In Petersville, there's just one street and no good restaurants. The only thing the town seems to have going for it is the rumor of delicious doughnuts that used to be made by Winnie, the owner of a local store. Tristan decides it's about time for the doughnuts to make a comeback, and he's the kid that's going to make that happen. Along with his new friend Josh—who's ready to help with a "how-to" book and lots of enthusiasm—the boys go about launching their baking business and bringing the magic back to Petersville.

QUICK LOOK

This book is about...

☆ Moving somewhere new
☆ Friendship

If you like this, check out...

☆ *Pie in the Sky*
  Pages 50-51
☆ *The A-Z Djinn Detective Agency*   Page 76

NEW KID
BY JERRY CRAFT

Jordan Banks isn't the only new kid at the fancy prep school his parents chose. But he is one of the few Black kids in his grade. Diverse? Not exactly.

All Jordan wants to do is go to art school. He has the talent—anyone who sees the cartoons he draws can tell that. But instead, thanks to his academics-focused mother, he's stuck at Riverdale Academy Day School. It's a place where his white teacher constantly calls him by the name of other Black boys, and he has to deal with bullies who don't seem to have any boundaries. Jordan faces a struggle to balance his new world at RAD and his old world at home in Washington Heights. Can he learn to like and stand up for the person he is growing into?

EXTRA INFO

This book is about...
☆ Growing pains
☆ The Black experience

If you like this, check out...
☆ *Prime Baby*
   Page 52
☆ *Ways to Make Sunshine*   Page 14

EFRÉN DIVIDED
BY ERNESTO CISNEROS

Efrén was born in America and is a citizen of the United States, but his parents are undocumented workers.

After a raid by the US immigration agency, Efrén's Amá is deported to Mexico. Now Efrén is in charge of taking care of his younger siblings as best as he can while also keeping up with school and helping around the house. Despite working overtime, Efrén's dad is struggling to get all the money he needs to bring Amá home. With his dad unable to take time off work, it's up to Efrén to travel to Tijuana to find his mother and deliver the money she needs to make her way back to the US—and her family.

EXTRA INFO

This book is about...

☆ Undocumented citizens
☆ Separated families

If you like this, check out...

☆ *Inside Out & Back Again*   Page 40
☆ *The Samosa Rebellion* Page 110

WINK
BY ROB HARRELL

When 12-year-old Ross loses his eye to cancer, he begins to worry about what else he might lose.

Things seem like they can't get much worse when one of Ross's friends ghosts him because he can't handle Ross's new situation and someone starts sending around mean cartoons about Ross's eye. However, things start to turn around when Ross decides to learn to play the guitar, and a new friendship starts to grow. With the help of his family, a team of medical geniuses, and a superhero pig, Ross realizes that being different isn't always a bad thing.

EXTRA INFO

This book is about...

☆ Being different

☆ Disability

If you like this, check out...

☆ *Show Me a Sign*
Page 59

☆ *The First Rule of Punk*
Page 29

SHOW ME A SIGN

BY ANN CLARE LEZOTTE

In the early 1800s, Mary Lambert lives in a community of islanders descended from English settlers who arrived at Martha's Vineyard and set up their own town of mostly deaf inhabitants.

The land where her village is used to belong to the Wampanoag people before it was unfairly sold off to the English. Now, tensions are running high between the Wampanoag people and the colonizers, and a tragedy in Mary's family shows her that her life on Martha's Vineyard isn't as complete as it once seemed. When Mary barely escapes becoming a sinister scientist's experiment, she is forced to come to terms with the way her community is perceived by outsiders seeking to harm them but also the harm the settlers caused to the Indigenous community they displaced, too.

EXTRA INFO

This book is about...

☆ Historical events

☆ Racism

If you like this, check out...

☆ *Indian No More*
Page 60

☆ *Maritcha: A Nineteenth-Century American Girl*
Page 66

INDIAN NO MORE

BY CHARLENE WILLING MCMANIS & TRACI SORELL

Overnight, 10-year-old Regina Petit goes from having a tribe and a home to having nothing.

When the US federal government decides that the Umpqua Tribe doesn't exist anymore, Regina's family are forced to move to Los Angeles as part of the Indian Relocation program—a program that moved Native Americans off their land and into urban areas. For the first time in her life, Regina is meeting people outside of her tribal community and facing hatred from people who want Native Americans to forget their histories and cultures and give up their land. In a new place with new friends, Regina must adjust to her new life without forgetting who she is and where she's from.

QUICK LOOK

This book is about...

☆ Displacement
☆ Indigenous culture

If you like this, check out...

☆ *Jo Jo Makoons: The Used-To-Be Best Friend*   Page 6
☆ *Other Words for Home*   Pages 42-43

THE NIGHT DIARY
BY VEERA HIRANANDANI

When her world is torn apart, Nisha must leave her home in Pakistan and travel on foot with her family to the house of an uncle she's never met.

In the diary she was given for her 12th birthday, Nisha documents all the changes in her life after the Partition of India in 1947. Nisha is half Muslim, half Hindu, and she's having a hard time trying to understand where she belongs now. With violence exploding between Muslims, Hindus, and Sikhs on the road to her uncle's and little food and no water, Nisha and her family face challenge after challenge as they seek safety and a new place to call home.

QUICK LOOK

This book is about...

☆ Displacement
☆ Family

If you like this, check out...

☆ *Nowhere Boy*
   Page 70

☆ *The Year of Goodbyes*
   Page 81

A GOOD KIND OF TROUBLE

BY LISA MOORE RAMÉE

When it comes to trouble, Shayla is happy to say a firm "no thank you!"

She doesn't want any trouble, and she doesn't need it. But when conversations about police brutality and the Black Lives Matter movement start to heat up around her family and friends, Shayla wonders if trouble might not be the only way to change the injustice she sees all around her. Following the lead of her big sister, Shayla decides to stand up against the racism at her school, even though not everyone understands why what she's doing is important. In the process, Shayla learns some big lessons about how important it is for all people to fight for justice.

QUICK LOOK

This book is about...

☆ Activism

☆ The Black experience

If you like this, check out...

☆ *Amal Unbound*
  Pages 64-65

☆ *Blended*
  Page 25

UNSPEAKABLE:
THE TULSA RACE MASSACRE

BY CAROLE BOSTON WEATHERFORD

In 1921, a community of middle-class Black people thrived in Greenwood, a 35-square block area in Tulsa, Oklahoma.

There were theaters, salons, hotels, libraries, a hospital, and newspapers all run by Black professionals to serve and support the Black community. This "Black Wall Street" showcased the successes of hardworking citizens who achieved as much as white people even in a segregated country. But when a Black man was accused of assaulting a white woman in an elevator, a mob of white people in Tulsa saw a perfect excuse to attack Greenwood. What followed was the deadliest racial massacre in US history. In little more than 24 hours, Greenwood was all but destroyed, its buildings torched and looted, and thousands of its citizens left homeless. This book documents one of the most destructive days in American history.

QUICK LOOK

This book is about...

⭐ Black history

⭐ Racism

If you like this, check out...

⭐ *Maritcha: A Nineteenth-Century American Girl* Page 66

⭐ *Roll Of Thunder, Hear My Cry* Page 87

AMAL UNBOUND
BY AISHA SAAED

Amal can't wait until she finishes school. She has big dreams of leaving her small town to go off to college and become a teacher.

However, after she accidentally offends her family's landlord, Amal is driven far away to a remote villa to work off her family's debt. Amal still has a strong spirit, and she makes friends with other servants at the house who—after a few hard conflicts—help her read and keep up with her education. When an opportunity presents itself to show everyone the cruelty of her family's landlord, it's up to Amal to have the courage to help set her family and friends free.

QUICK LOOK

This book is about...

☆ Girl power
☆ Girls' rights

If you like this, check out...

☆ *Malala: My Story of Standing Up for Girls' Rights* Page 114
☆ *Rolling Warrior* Page 17

AUTHOR INTERVIEW

What inspired you to write this book?

Amal's story is set in a village in Pakistan, and those are my own ancestral roots. I remember playing in my grandfather's sugarcane fields and orange groves. I remember the lively markets, colorful clothing, and delicious food. I wanted to bring this world to readers.

How did you create the main character in this book?

Amal was inspired, in part, by Pakistani Nobel Peace Prize winner Malala Yousefzai. She risked her life speaking out for education equality. I wanted to write a story about a brave girl who also took risks, who may not become famous but whose work mattered all the same.

Where did you write this book? At home? A coffee shop? The library?

I get distracted pretty easily, so the best place for me to write is in a quiet place in my house. My writing spot is a cozy nook in the corner of my bedroom where I have lots of notebooks, my computer, and plenty of tea.

What tips do you have for young writers?

If you want to be a writer some day, the best way to grow your skills is to read! I read at least 50 books each year, and I reread books I love so I can both enjoy them again and also learn how to be a better writer.

How do you keep going when you get stuck/writing gets hard?

When I get stuck, I take a deep breath and remind myself that it's normal to feel this way sometimes.

ABOUT THE AUTHOR

Aisha Saaed can speak three languages fluently—English, Punjabi, and Urdu. Her favorite country is Turkey, and she is afraid of heights. She lives with her family in Atlanta, Georgia.

What's your favorite word?

"Joy" is my favorite word. Every day there can be so many different things that don't go our way, but every day there are also so many small lovely moments that we can find a moment of joy in. Joy is an important part of my writing experience.

MARITCHA: A NINETEENTH-CENTURY AMERICAN GIRL

BY TONYA BOLDEN

At the end of her life, Maritcha Lyons—a free Black girl—left an unfinished memoir. This biographical account of her life is based on that memoir.

It tells the story of a little girl growing up in New York just before the Civil War and Reconstruction. Born to working-class but influential parents, Maritcha and her siblings live a vibrant life. They are free, but elsewhere in the US, slavery continues, as Maritcha knows only too well. The Lyons' home is filled with friends, family, and boarders, but they also welcome runaway enslaved people too, along with dignitaries and abolitionists. After violence pushes her out of New York, the teenage Maritcha follows through on the activism of her parents and their friends. She successfully integrates a school in Providence, becoming its first-ever Black graduate.

QUICK LOOK

This book is about...

⭐ Activism

⭐ Black history

If you like this, check out...

⭐ *All Thirteen*
Pages 118-119

⭐ *The Year of Goodbyes*
Page 81

FREE LUNCH
BY REX OGLE

Twelve-year-old Rex is always working. Always. And that doesn't just mean schoolwork.

Rex's home life is filled with cooking, taking care of his baby brother, and dodging beatings from his stepfather and mother. Starting middle school should be a welcome break, but it only adds to his worries. That's because Rex is the poor biracial kid in a class of rich kids, and seemingly the only one in the free lunch program. Rex tries his best to swallow the shame and hold his head high, but it's hard, especially when friends start to fade away, and he has to deal with bullying from his English teacher and a wealthy neighborhood troublemaker. But a new friendship helps Rex to start feeling more hopeful.

QUICK LOOK

This book is about...

☆ Friendship

☆ Poverty

If you like this, check out...

☆ *Efrén Divided*
Page 57

☆ *Merci Suárez Changes Gears* Pages 18-19

THE 1619 PROJECT: BORN ON THE WATER

BY NIKOLE HANNAH-JONES & RENÉE WATSON

Short, rhythmic poems trace the origins of enslaved Africans from the Kingdom of Ndongo in West Central Africa to the shores of 1619 Virginia.

In these haunting verses, an amazing tale unfolds—the tale of the ancestors who gave birth to the first African Americans. In Africa, they had knowledge, power, joy, beautiful languages, and rich histories. But that was all taken from them when they were stolen from their lands and carried across the Atlantic Ocean on a ship named *The White Lion.* Far from their countries, their families, and everything they knew, they would now be forced to help build a New World for white colonizers. These poems show how—despite losing their homes—the new arrivals found ways to survive, how they fought, and how they continue to fight for their freedom today.

QUICK LOOK

This book is about...
☆ Black history
☆ Slavery

If you like this, check out...
☆ *Starfish*
Page 21
☆ *The House of Dies Drear*   Page 105

THE STORY OF THE WINDRUSH
BY K. N. CHIMBIRI

After World War II, hundreds of hopeful Black people traveled from different islands in the Caribbean to the UK seeking jobs and new experiences. These are some of their stories.

Musicians, soldiers, and so many more share their dreams about what life would be like for them in the UK. While some of the new arrivals were able to find work before or soon after they arrived, still more citizens faced—and continue to face—racism that stopped them from having the life they imagined on the journey over aboard the HMS *Windrush*. Readers get an opportunity to meet members of an incredible generation whose skills and community helped shape the UK as we now know it.

QUICK LOOK

This book is about...

⭐ Black history

⭐ Immigration

If you like this, check out...

⭐ *The Boy Who Harnessed the Wind*   Page 116

⭐ *Unspeakable: The Tulsa Race Massacre*   Page 63

NOWHERE BOY

BY KATHERINE MARSH

Ahmed and Max are from different worlds. When events beyond Ahmed's control put him in danger, will Max find the courage to do what's right?

In Brussels, two kids new to the city forge an unlikely friendship. Ahmed is a Syrian refugee who has suffered more loss in his early years than anyone should have to in a lifetime. Max is a 13-year-old white American who can't quite get the language right. Bonding over their love of superhero comics, the friends soon learn a painful lesson: Life sometimes demands heroics of the most un-super people. Keeping Ahmed safe from those who want to hurt him because he's Muslim will require both friends to find extraordinary amounts of courage. And they won't have capes, weapons, or superpowers to help them.

QUICK LOOK

This book is about...
☆ Displacement
☆ Friendship

If you like this, check out...
☆ *Other Words for Home*   Pages 42-43
☆ *The Night Diary* Page 61

HOLES

BY LOUIS SACHAR

Stanley Yelnats didn't steal any stinking sneakers!

But the police and judge don't care when he's caught red-handed with the cleats of a famous baseball player. They send Stanley off to Camp Green Lake where all he does all day long is dig holes where the lake used to be. When Stanley starts digging up more than holes, he sets off a chain of events involving breaking curses, a bid for freedom, and... pigs. He doesn't know it, but he could be the key to ending the Yelnats family's run of bad luck that started more than 100 years ago.

QUICK LOOK

This book is about...

☆ Family

☆ Fate and destiny

If you like this, check out...

☆ *From the Desk of Zoe Washington*   Page 74

☆ *Hello, Universe* Pages 88-89

FROM THE MIXED-UP FILES OF MRS. BASIL E. FRANKWEILER

BY E. L. KONIGSBURG

Claudia Kincaid is totally fed up with not being appreciated at home, so she comes up with a genius plan to run away to New York City—the Metropolitan Museum of Art to be exact.

But Claudia has one problem—the little bit of money she has won't get her very far. Fortunately, her younger brother Jamie is the perfect runaway partner, because (1) He won't tell, and (2) He's rich. Once they're at the Met, the siblings get caught up in the mystery of Angel, a beautiful marble sculpture sold to the museum by the mysterious Mrs. Basil E. Frankweiler. Claudia and Jamie are determined to find out whether Angel was really created by the famous artist Michaelangelo, and Claudia won't return home until she knows—even if that means having to confront Mrs. Basil E. Frankweiler herself!

QUICK LOOK

This book is about...

☆ Secrets

☆ Siblings

If you like this, check out...

☆ *High-Rise Mystery*
   Page 75

☆ *Lily & Kosmo in Outer Outer Space*   Page 33

AMARI AND THE NIGHT BROTHERS
BY B. B. ALSTON

After her brother Quinton disappears, Amari is surprised to learn that he has put her name forward to compete for a place at the Bureau of Supernatural Affairs—the same secret training program he was in.

When Amari learns that Quinton was one of the Bureau's most famous agents who disappeared on the job, she's willing to do anything to stay close to the Bureau—even if that means spending the summer in a camp working to become a Junior Agent herself. Along the way, Amari discovers that if you have the right eyewear, it's easy to see that many of the mythical and magical beings we think are imaginary are very real and living in the world with us. Now that she knows anything is possible, Amari is more determined than ever to find out what happened to Quinton.

QUICK LOOK

This book is about...

☆ Family
☆ Intergalactic adventures

If you like this, check out...

☆ *City of Ghosts*
Pages 100–101

☆ *The Missing Piece of Charlie O'Reilly*   Page 79

FROM THE DESK OF ZOE WASHINGTON

BY JANAE MARKS

On her 12th birthday, Zoe Washington gets a letter from her dad, Marcus, who she hasn't seen since she was little.

He's writing from prison to tell Zoe that he didn't commit the crime he is accused of, but Zoe's mom is not interested in her daughter getting to know Marcus at all. Even though Zoe's got an important baking competition coming up, she's determined to help clear her father's name and win the competition with her creative cupcake recipe. There's a lot that must be done in order to prove Marcus's innocence, and Zoe might be alone in her fight to clear her dad's name.

QUICK LOOK

This book is about...
☆ Family
☆ Racism

If you like this, check out...
☆ *Fast Pitch*
Page 85
☆ *Holes*
Page 71

HIGH-RISE MYSTERY

BY SHARNA JACKSON

Nik and Norva are sister detectives determined to find out who killed their art teacher.

The girls love their estate—The Triangle—in southeast London. It's a tight-knit community where they know everything about everyone. Or at least they thought they did, until they discover their art teacher Hugo's body in the trash room of their high-rise building. Now it's up to them to find out what happened to Hugo so that their dad doesn't go down for the crime. Nik's thoughtful approach and Norva's gutsy detective styles can sometimes prove tricky to balance, but the sibling detectives follow every action-packed turn to a truly twisted ending.

QUICK LOOK

This book is about...

☆ Family

☆ The Black experience

If you like this, check out...

☆ *From the Desk of Zoe Washington*   Page 74

☆ *One Crazy Summer* Page 16

THE A–Z DJINN DETECTIVE AGENCY

BY PARINITA SHETTY

Ashwin has only two months to get enough rupees to pay for his class trip to Gujarat.

There's no way his mother would be able to give him the money for the trip, so it's up to Ashwin to come up with a plan to earn the money. When he finds a spell to summon a djinn, it seems like all Ashwin's problems are solved. But when the djinn, Zubeida, appears, it turns out that she's just a kid like him. And she can't grant him money. What she can do, though, is shapeshift and turn invisible. *Sort of.* At least invisible enough to help Ashwin start a detective agency that will help people solve their problems from A to Z. *Sort of.*

QUICK LOOK

This book is about...

☆ Friendship

☆ Indian culture

If you like this, check out...

☆ *Agent Zaiba Investigates: The Missing Diamonds*   Page 78

☆ *Jupiter Storm*
Page 15

ANISHA, ACCIDENTAL DETECTIVE

BY SERENA PATEL

Anisha is not super excited about her Aunty Bindi's wedding, but that doesn't mean she wanted the groom to get kidnapped!

Everyone in Anisha's house is already worried about the wedding, so when Anisha gets a note saying that her soon-to-be Uncle Tony is in trouble, Anisha knows it's better that she investigates without the adults knowing. She grabs her animal-obsessed best friend Milo, and together, they follow clues that lead them all over Anisha's backyard, neighborhood, and even her school! When the adults finally discover that Uncle Tony is missing, the pressure is on Anisha to find him and save her Aunty Bindi's big day!

QUICK LOOK

This book is about...

☆ Family

☆ Hindu culture

If you like this, check out...

☆ *Agent Zaiba Investigates: The Missing Diamonds* Page 78

☆ *Planet Omar: Accidental Trouble Magnet* Page 46

AGENT ZAIBA INVESTIGATES: THE MISSING DIAMONDS

BY ANNABELLE SAMI

Zaiba is ready to be known as the best detective in the world.

When a famous actress's dog disappears from the hotel where Zaiba's cousin is having her Mehndi party, it's Zaiba's chance to show everyone what a super sleuth she is. Lucky for Zaiba, investigating is in her blood—her aunt is a detective in Pakistan. Zaiba must use every book and idea her aunt has ever given her to help crack the case. With the help of her best friend Poppy and little brother Ali, Zaiba is ready to solve the mystery and bring home the dog—and its collar full of diamonds!

QUICK LOOK

This book is about...
☆ Girl power
☆ Pakistani culture

If you like this, check out...
☆ *Danny Chung Does Not Do Maths*   Page 86
☆ *Jupiter Storm*   Page 15

THE MISSING PIECE OF CHARLIE O'REILLY

BY REBECCA K.S. ANSARI

When Charlie wishes for his own room without his annoying little brother Liam, he's surprised to wake up the next morning to find that Liam is gone.

Even more surprising is that no one even remembers Charlie having a little brother. Not his mom. Not his dad. Not even his best friend, Ana. Luckily, even though she doesn't remember Liam, Ana is willing to help Charlie find out what happened to him. The search for Liam leads them to an old asylum where kids who have been wished away are being held. But while there, Charlie and Ana unlock more secrets about Charlie's family and their connection to the asylum than he ever could have imagined.

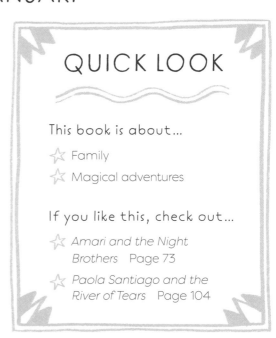

QUICK LOOK

This book is about...

☆ Family

☆ Magical adventures

If you like this, check out...

☆ *Amari and the Night Brothers*   Page 73

☆ *Paola Santiago and the River of Tears*   Page 104

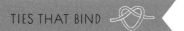

THE SEASON OF STYX MALONE
BY KEKLA MAGOON

Brothers Caleb and Bobby Gene Franklin are ready for an adventure-filled summer in the woods behind their house.

The thing is, Caleb wants something bigger and more magical than anything their little town of Sutton, Indiana, has ever seen before. Enter 16-year-old Styx Malone and his grand promises. When Styx tells Caleb and Bobby Gene that he can turn an old sack of fireworks into a moped, the boys are willing to risk everything in order to see Styx do something that is seemingly impossible. Caleb and Bobby Gene follow Styx everywhere, from jumping onto freight trains to being by their new friend's side when he's rushed to the hospital. But they begin to realize that sometimes magic isn't worth all the trouble.

QUICK LOOK

This book is about...

☆ Adventure

☆ Friendship

If you like this, check out...

☆ *High-Rise Mystery*
Page 75

☆ *Jupiter Storm*
Page 15

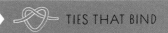

THE YEAR OF GOODBYES

BY DEBBIE LEVY

Twelve-year-old Jutta is a Jewish girl living in Germany during the 1930s. This book is written by her daughter and is based on the experiences Jutta recorded in a photobook.

The poetry fully captures the experiences of a young girl whose childhood is interrupted by the rise of Adolf Hitler's Nazi party and the Holocaust. Filled the year before Jutta escaped with her family to the US, her photobook is the inspiration for her daughter's poem, and mingled with the poetry are photos and hopeful quotations from Jutta's friends and family. A timeline also tracks Jutta's amazing story alongside key events of the era, enabling readers to connect more deeply with Jutta's experience.

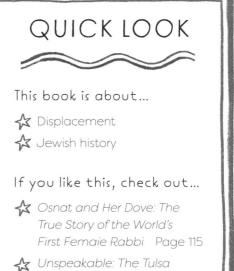

QUICK LOOK

This book is about...

⭐ Displacement

⭐ Jewish history

If you like this, check out...

⭐ *Osnat and Her Dove: The True Story of the World's First Femaie Rabbi*   Page 115

⭐ *Unspeakable: The Tulsa Race Massacre*   Page 63

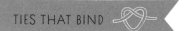

TWO NAOMIS

BY OLUGBEMISOLA RHUDAY-PERKOVICH

The only thing that Naomi Marie and Naomi Edith have in common is their name. Or so they think.

Each girl is also dealing with her parents' divorce and changes to her family. Naomi Edith is living with her dad after her mom moves across the country to take a job in California. And even though Naomi Marie's dad lives nearby, he's definitely not getting back together with her mom. In fact, Naomi Marie's mom is now dating Naomi Edith's dad, and the parents really want the two Naomis to get along. When they both join a coding class for girls, Naomi Marie and Naomi Edith start to realize that maybe sharing their lives—and their families—might not be such a terrible thing after all.

QUICK LOOK

This book is about...

☆ Changing families

☆ Friendship

If you like this, check out...

☆ *Blended*
Page 25

☆ *One Crazy Summer*
Page 16

AUTHOR INTERVIEW

How did you create the main character in this book?

I wrote *Two Naomis* with my good friend Audrey Vernick. We wrote two main characters: Naomi Marie and Naomi E. I wrote from Naomi Marie's point of view, and I had a lot of fun coming up with this girl who was very much a big sister and an "organizer." She felt very clear about who she was and what she was about, and then having Naomi E. come into her life really threw her for a loop! I drew from a lot of how I was as a slightly bossy older sister, and she took on a life of her own from there. I spend a lot of time thinking about my characters, imagining them in different situations and scenarios.

Where did you write this book? At home? A coffee shop? The library?

I work from home, but I really love working at the different branch libraries of the Brooklyn and New York Public Library systems. Each one has a personality and a vibrancy of its own. And whenever I need inspiration, I'm surrounded by great books!

What tips do you have for young writers?

I think that reading and studying the stories that you love can help you with your writing. Look at what the storytellers that you respect and admire do, and think about why and how they do it. Reading your work aloud can be very helpful. Let your listener ask questions. See where they're confused, where they're excited, and ask them what they're connected to.

How do you keep going when you get stuck/writing gets hard?

Sometimes I take a walk—that's a big part of my writing process. Walking often "unlocks" something that helps me think through a story problem.

ABOUT THE AUTHOR

Olugbemisola Rhuday-Perkovich was the "new kid" at school lots of times. She now lives in New York City with her family. She loves crafting and would like to see all the subway art in her city.

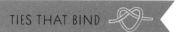
BROWN GIRL DREAMING

BY JACQUELINE WOODSON

From Ohio to South Carolina and on to New York City, Jackie's life is one of constant movement. As a poet, she has a lot to say about the journey.

In 1963, when Jackie is born, the US is struggling with issues of race, gender, and equality. Times are changing for everyone, but for Jackie, places are changing, too. First, she swaps life in the Midwest for the slow-moving South, before moving to fast-paced Brooklyn. As a kid, Jackie finds that writing helps her make sense of the sometimes scary world she's in and the often complicated family she's getting to know. In this collection of poems, Jackie beautifully describes time with her grandparents enjoying nature in the American South, having fun with her new best friend, Maria, in Brooklyn, and the moments—good and bad—that make her the grown-up dreamer she is today.

QUICK LOOK

This book is about...

★ Family

★ The Black experience

If you like this, check out...

★ *Out of Wonder*
Page 24

★ *Roll of Thunder, Hear My Cry*   Page 87

FAST PITCH

BY NIC STONE

The Fulton Firebirds is an all Black softball team competing for the regional championship in a mainly white league.

Twelve-year-old Shenice Lockwood is the Firebirds' captain, and she's determined to lead her team to victory. But it's a little hard for her to concentrate on softball when she meets her great-uncle Jack and learns about her grandfather—a sporting legend who Jack says was framed for a crime that ruined his chances at the big leagues. Now Shenice has two things to worry about: winning the regional championship AND clearing her great-grandfather's name. As Shenice tries to uncover the family mystery, she learns that she's more than good enough to be on any field as a leader and a player, no matter how much other people may try to shut her—or her forefathers—out.

QUICK LOOK

This book is about...

☆ Family
☆ Solving mysteries

If you like this, check out...

☆ *Holes*
Page 71

☆ *The Magic in Changing Your Stars* Page 32

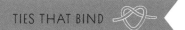

DANNY CHUNG DOES NOT DO MATHS

BY MAISIE CHAN

All Danny Chung wants is to draw his super awesome comics and have sleepovers on his new bunk bed with his best friend Sir Ravi.

But that's going to be awfully hard now that—SURPRISE!—his grandma Nai Nai is moving in on the top bunk. While Nai Nai's adjusting to her new life in England, Danny's stuck stopping her from bowling with citrus fruits and walking on walls. But when it becomes clear that Nai Nai is a secret math genius—something Danny definitely isn't—Danny realizes just how important friendship and family is, no matter your age or talent.

QUICK LOOK

This book is about...

☆ Chinese culture
☆ Family

If you like this check out...

☆ *Anisha, Accidental Detective*   Page 77
☆ *Merci Suárez Changes Gears*   Pages 18-19

ROLL OF THUNDER, HEAR MY CRY

BY MILDRED D. TAYLOR

Together with her family, smart and bold Cassie Logan stands up to the hurtful racism of white people in her small Mississippi town.

Racism runs deep in the community where the Logans tend their farm. The family bear it with dignity, but sometimes bearing things is not enough. When three local Black men are set on fire, the Logans ask their neighbors to come together and boycott the store of the white men who committed the crimes. The response leaves them feeling let down, and Cassie wondering just how much pain and sorrow they can take. When her family and some of their neighbors become targets for deep hatred, they begin to stand up for themselves. Deciding to fight back is tough, but the alternative is worse—to give up and accept the racism that threatens them all.

QUICK LOOK

This book is about...

⭐ Family
⭐ Racism

If you like this, check out...

⭐ *Amina's Voice*
Page 23

⭐ *A Single Shard*
Page 36-37

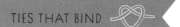

HELLO, UNIVERSE
BY ERIN ENTRADA KELLY

Shy Virgil Salinas feels out of place everywhere.

At school, he can't get up the courage to talk to his crush—the cool and confident Valencia. And at home, his multigenerational Filipino family are loving but hard to connect with sometimes. When Chet, the neighborhood bully, pulls a mean prank, Virgil ends up trapped at the bottom of a well with only his guinea pig for company. The universe brings Valencia and self-proclaimed kid psychic Kaori together to that same well, and as each character shares some of their story, we learn about their struggle to be the person they want and need to be.

QUICK LOOK

This book is about...

☆ Fitting in

☆ Friendship

If you like this, check out...

☆ *Look Both Ways: A Tale Told in Ten Blocks*   Page 92-93

☆ *So Done*
Page 94

AUTHOR INTERVIEW

What inspired you to write this book?

I wanted to write about a shy, sensitive boy. I wanted to celebrate Filipino folklore and family. I wanted a character who told fortunes. And I wanted to explore a timeless question: Are our lives driven by fate or coincidence?

How did you create the main character in this book?

I ask my characters lots of questions before I get started, like: What are you afraid of? What do you want most? Who—or what—do you love most in the world? How do you view yourself? How do others view you? On and on and on. I interrogate my characters until I know them better than they know themselves.

Where did you write this book? At home? A coffee shop? The library?

I do most of my writing at home, in a notebook. I also love writing in libraries. I can't write in coffee shops—too many distractions.

What tips do you have for young writers?

Read often and write often. It's okay if you start stories and never finish them. One day, you'll find a story that won't let go, and you'll finish it. Sometimes we abandon projects until we find the right one.

How do you keep going when you get stuck/writing gets hard?

When I get stuck, I do something else. I read a lot. I especially love reading nonfiction when I'm working on a novel—something totally different from what I'm working on. I also love playing piano.

ABOUT THE AUTHOR

Erin Entrada Kelly is a FilipinaAmerican author and illustrator. Her favorite season is spring, and she loves scary movies.

What was your favorite middle-grade book as a kid?

I loved Judy Blume. I loved *Sideways Stories from Wayside School* by Louis Sachar. And I loved *Halfway Down Paddy Lane* by Jean Marzollo.

What's your favorite word?

"Peculiar" rolls off the tongue in an interesting way. There's mystery behind the word "peculiar." If someone says, "Hm, that's peculiar," you're instantly curious. Speaking of which, "curious" is another great word. I like how Alice uses it—"Curiouser and curiouser."

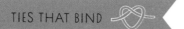
HURRICANE CHILD
BY KACEN CALLENDER

Caroline Murphy cannot catch a break.

When Caroline's mom takes off to travel the world, she leaves Caroline and her father behind on their Caribbean island. Every day feels like a battle at school and at home. Everyone thinks Caroline is bad luck because she was born during a hurricane. Between the bullying, the absent mother, and the woman in black haunting her, Caroline is starting to believe she is bad luck, too. But when Caroline makes friends with Kalinda—the new kid at school—her luck starts to change, and the girls are surprised to find that more than friendship is blooming between them.

QUICK LOOK

This book is about...
☆ LGBTQ+
☆ Missing parent

If you like this, check out...
☆ *Hoodoo*
   Pages 106-107
☆ *The Jumbies*
   Page 102

ME, MY DAD AND THE END OF THE RAINBOW

BY BENJAMIN DEAN

In the "Before Days"—before they decided to divorce, that is—Archie's parents were deeply in love.

But now they're not, and it's turning Archie's world upside down. When Archie's dad reveals that he's gay, Archie decides to head to London Pride with his friends Seb and Bell to learn how to support his dad. At Pride, the trio meet people from all over the LGBTQ+ community and learn that family can be people who are related to you or people you choose. But the most important thing is that there's love and care in the mix!

QUICK LOOK

This book is about...

☆ LGBTQ+

☆ Changing families

If you like this, check out...

☆ *Hurricane Child*
  Page 90

☆ *The Insiders*
  Pages 26-27

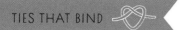

LOOK BOTH WAYS: A TALE TOLD IN TEN BLOCKS

BY JASON REYNOLDS

At Latimer Middle School, there are many paths home. As many different paths as there are cool kids to walk them.

Ten trips home from school. Ten different stories to tell. Whether they're silly, sentimental, or thought-provoking, these stories all combine into one important picture—a picture of kids with big personalities. The story of best friends catching up after one of them returns to school after struggling with their health somehow fits perfectly with another about classmates discussing where boogers come from. Confessons about awkward crushes and truly terrible advice mingle with quests for the best routes for avoiding the scariest dogs. In fact, there's only one thing these 10 tales have in common. They're all about unique kids being uniquely kids.

QUICK LOOK

This book is about...

☆ Friendship
☆ Growing pains

If you like this, check out...

☆ *Out of Wonder*
Page 24
☆ *The Last Last-Day-Of-Summer*   Page 53

AUTHOR INTERVIEW

How did you create the main character in this book?

I don't know if there is a main character. And if there is one, it would probably have to be the school bus, which happens to be falling from the sky. How did I create that? Well... I vowed to never tell.

Where did you write this book? At home? A coffee shop? The library?

I actually wrote this in a bed-and-breakfast in Cambridge, Massachusetts, in between teaching MFA classes. I can't explain it, but just know this book poured out of me. It's like every one of these characters had been living under my tongue for years.

What tips do you have for young writers?

Make the thing you want to make. I repeat, make the thing YOU want to make.

What was the process like in getting this book published?

I mean, I'm a little spoiled at this point because I just make what I want and turn it in. From there, usually, we start the editorial process, which can sometimes be brutal. But this time in particular, my first draft was pretty clean. Sometimes it happens that way.

How do you keep going when you get stuck/writing gets hard?

I have a theory about how to unstick a story, and I'm not saying it always works, but it works most of the time—character or characteristic. What does this mean? It means when you're stuck, sometimes the story is asking for there to be a new character introduced to shake things up. Other times, the story is asking that your main character has an extra characteristic that could open unexplored plotlines.

ABOUT THE AUTHOR

Jason Reynolds was inspired by rap to start writing poetry, but he never read a book from beginning to end until he was 17. He now lives in Washington D.C., and is a collector of African American bookish memorabilia.

What was your favorite middle-grade book as a kid?

There's nothing I can remember reading, because reading wasn't my thing. But I do remember thinking *How to Eat Fried Worms* sounded interesting. Never read it, but, sheesh... what an amazing title!

What's your favorite word?

So many! Enthusiasm. Stumblebum. Triage. Strangely, those three kind of work in tandem. HA!

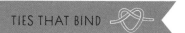
SO DONE

BY PAULA CHASE

When Tai's best friend Mila comes home after staying with her aunt over the summer, she's acting really funny, and Tai doesn't like it.

While both Mila and Tai know that big changes are coming once they move into the eighth grade—especially since there's a new program starting at their school—they're handling things differently. Mila wants to concentrate on her dancing, while Tai starts to fall in with the kids who hang around their community. Tai is worried about the distance that seems to be growing between them, but she has no idea how to fill the space. When she learns the truth about why Mila is pulling away, it may be too big for her to get back the only best friend she's ever had.

QUICK LOOK

This book is about...
☆ Changing friendships
☆ Growing pains

If you like this, check out...
☆ *Amina's Voice*
   Page 23
☆ *The Moon Within*
   Page 20

THE GRAVEYARD BOOK

BY NEIL GAIMAN

Bod isn't dead, but he does live in a graveyard and is always surrounded by ghosts.

After his whole family was murdered when he was a baby, Bod escaped to the graveyard near his old house, where he has lived ever since. Now that he's older, it's almost time for him to leave the safety of the graveyard—and his vampire guardian Silas—behind. The only thing stopping him is the killer who is still looking for the child who got away all those years ago. A beautiful ghost story about love, loss, and revenge.

QUICK LOOK

This book is about...

☆ Losing family
☆ Growing up different

If you like this, check out...

☆ *Holes*
   Page 71
☆ *Spirit Hunters*
   Page 96

SPIRIT HUNTERS

BY ELLEN OH

Harper's big move from New York to Washington D.C., is pretty scary, but it's nothing compared to what goes on in her family's new haunted house!

It doesn't take long for Harper to sense something wrong in her new home. She soon learns that, for decades, unexplainable events and tragedies have been happening there. When her little brother makes an invisible—and dangerous—new friend, Harper slowly realizes this may not be the first time their family has encountered bad spirits. But what's to be done? With her mom not interested in ghost stories, her older sister more concerned with being a teenager, and her dad only a little sympathetic, it's up to Harper to figure out what to do. With the help of friends and her Grandma Lee, Harper goes all out to save her brother—and the day—in this haunting ghost story.

QUICK LOOK

This book is about...

☆ Family
☆ Supernatural adventures

If you like this, check out...

☆ *The House of Dies Drear*   Page 105
☆ *The Missing Piece of Charlie O'Reilly*   Page 79

JUST SOUTH OF HOME

BY KAREN STRONG

Sarah's cousin Janie is visiting for the summer, and her bad behavior is stirring up supernatural trouble in Sarah's small Georgia town.

When Janie steals from a haunted church, the quiet summer Sarah was hoping for melts away like an ice-cream cone. Now she's stuck trying to help the spirits of long-dead folks find peace in their afterlives. To do that, the town must face the racism that took the lives of many people and tore the community apart. If Sarah can't get the townspeople, including her super religious grandma, to confront their past before it's too late, her family— and the souls of the spirits—will never have peace.

QUICK LOOK

This book is about...

☆ Black history
☆ Family

If you like this, check out...

☆ *A Kind of Spark*
  Page 28

☆ *Zombierella: Fairy Tales Gone Bad* Page 98

ZOMBIERELLA: FAIRY TALES GONE BAD

BY JOSEPH COELHO

When Cinderella slips and falls down the stairs before a ball, Death swoops in to... save her life?

SURPRISE! Death doesn't exactly bring Cinderella back to the land of the living. Instead, he turns her into Zombierella and allows her to go to the ball to dance and make merry with the Prince. When Zombierella flees at midnight, the smitten Prince must use the one thing she left behind—a body part—to try to find his true love. With some great gore and tight poetry, this is a delightfully twisted fairy tale.

QUICK LOOK

This book is about...

☆ Alternative fairy tales
☆ Girl power

If you like this, check out...

☆ *Osnat and Her Dove: The True Story of the World's First Female Rabbi*   Page 115
☆ *The Princess in Black* Page 109

GHOST SQUAD
BY CLARIBEL A. ORTEGA

Most of Lucely Luna's family are ghosts, but it's far from scary. In fact, it's great!

When Lucely's family members die, they don't go away. They become firefly spirits living in the willow tree in her yard, so they're still around to protect and guide Lucely. Except, perhaps, when they're taking a break to enjoy a delicious breakfast served up by her ghost tour-leading dad! One day, the firefly lights start to flicker and dim, and Lucely knows that something is very wrong. She teams up with her best friend Syd and Syd's witch (seriously!) grandmother, Babette, to fight an invasion of evil spirits. Together with a deep-voiced cat, the three of them become the Ghost Squad. Armed with ghost catchers to banish the spirits and their personalized jackets, they're out to save not just Lucely's family but the entire city.

QUICK LOOK

This book is about...

⭐ Family

⭐ Supernatural adventures

If you like this, check out...

⭐ *Dragons in a Bag*
Page 35

⭐ *Sam Wu is Not Afraid of Ghosts*   Page 54

CITY OF GHOSTS
BY VICTORIA SCHWAB

Cassidy didn't have a "near-death experience." She had an actual death experience. Kind of.

Luckily, she was pulled back from the Veil—the gateway that separates the land of the living from the dead—by her best friend Jacob, who is actually dead. Being best friends with a ghost has its perks, especially when Cass travels to Edinburgh with her ghost hunter parents, who have no idea they're being haunted by her BFF. There, she meets Lara, who can also see ghosts. Now the trio must take on a soul-snatching villain feeding on kids in one of the most haunted cities in the world.

QUICK LOOK

This book is about...

⭐ Creepy places
⭐ Friendship

If you like this, check out...

⭐ *Paola Santiago and the River of Tears*   Page 104

⭐ *The Graveyard Book* Page 95

AUTHOR INTERVIEW

What inspired you to write this book?

I actually live in Edinburgh, Scotland, and one of my favorite things is that it's not only a city with so much history, but a very haunted one! Everyone you meet can tell you at least one ghost story about Edinburgh, and they tell it as if they were talking about something their aunt did once—it's almost normal. It's so much a part of the place, and I love the idea that ghost stories are tied to a physical location—it means that everywhere is haunted, because everywhere has its own history. City of Ghosts gave me the chance to tell a central ghost story—Cassidy's—but also some of the real ghost stories that belong to the city where the book is set!

What tips do you have for young writers?

Get the story down on paper. Don't worry about making it perfect; just focus on finishing it. Getting to the end without abandoning the work is the hardest part, but once you get there, you can make it better. The one thing you can't fix is a blank page.

How do you keep going when you get stuck/writing gets hard?

I get overwhelmed really easily, but I've discovered that for me, the secrets are: (1) Breaking the work down into the smallest bites possible, and (2) Remembering that I'm not writing a whole book in that moment, only a sentence, a paragraph, a scene. One thing that helps when I get stuck is creating a two to four sentence summary of what I want to happen in the scene. Then I see if I can expand that to six sentences. eight sentences. ten sentences. Now, can I write a line that excites me?

ABOUT THE AUTHOR

Victoria "V.E." Schwab is the #1 *New York Times* bestselling author of the acclaimed *Shades of Magic* series and the international bestseller *The Invisible Life of Addie LaRue*. She lives in Edinbugh and is usually tucked in the corner of a coffee shop dreaming up monsters.

What's a middle-grade book that you wish you had written and why?

I love many books but don't often wish I'd written them. The one exception? *The Graveyard Book* by Neil Gaiman. It's not only exquisite, but it has all my favorite themes, and it handles them so elegantly.

THE JUMBIES

BY TRACEY BAPTISTE

Eleven-year-old Corinne La Mer is not impressed by Severine, the new, beautiful stranger who has just strolled into town.

There's something about Severine that makes Corinne shiver, but she refuses to believe that Severine could be a jumbie—until Severine tries to turn Corinne's dad into a jumbie, too! Corinne teams up with her new friend Dru and brothers Boukie and Malik to defend their island against a Jumbie takeover. However, once the fighting starts, Corinne learns more about the land they all live on, who it belonged to first, and how the compassion and courage of one person can plant a seed for peace that will grow to save them all.

QUICK LOOK

This book is about...

☆ Carribean folklore

☆ Family

If you like this, check out...

☆ *Ghost Squad*
  Page 99

☆ *Small Spaces*
  Page 103

SMALL SPACES

BY KATHERINE ARDEN

After Ollie's mom dies, she turns to books to feel better.

When she gets hold of a book under strange circumstances, Ollie never could have imagined it would mean that she'd have to outwit the villain in the book, known only as the smiling man. But that's exactly what happens! Ollie joins forces with her classmates Coco and Brian, and the trio must duck ghosts and creepy scarecrows in order to keep themselves safe from the smiling man. The only thing they know they must do? Stay in small spaces.

QUICK LOOK

This book is about...

☆ Loss of a parent
☆ Creepy places

If you like this, check out...

☆ *Amari and the Night Brothers*   Page 73
☆ *City of Ghosts* Pages 100-101

PAOLA SANTIAGO AND THE RIVER OF TEARS

BY TEHLOR KAY MEJIA

Paola Santiago's superstitious mom never allowed her to go to the river—even before the drowning.

She was always warning Paola about La Llorona—the mysterious woman who drags kids to their deaths in the water. After one of their classmates drowns in the Gila River where they hang out, Paola and her friends Dante and Emma decide it's probably best to keep their time dreaming and laughing on its banks a secret. But when Emma goes missing, Paola and Dante must enter the Rift—a world where their parents' myths and monsters are very, very real—in order to bring Emma home.

QUICK LOOK

This book is about...

⭐ Latinx folklore
⭐ Friendship

If you like this, check out...

⭐ *Healer of the Water Monster*   Page 108
⭐ *The Jumbies* Page 102

THE HOUSE OF DIES DREAR
BY VIRGINIA HAMILTON

As soon as he sees the house of abolitionist Dies Drear, Thomas Smalls knows there's something haunted about it.

Thomas and his family moved into the house so that his professor dad can study its history. But strange things keep happening around the whole Smalls family, and the house's caretaker—the mysterious Mr. Pluto—only adds to the spooky feeling. Who are the people Thomas sees on the property, and what do they want? While his father is learning about the house's history as a stop on the Underground Railroad, Thomas tries to unwrap the secrets of its past in other ways, and he discovers that there's much more to the legends and stories about Dies Drear than he ever expected.

QUICK LOOK

This book is about...

☆ Black history
☆ Haunted places

If you like this, check out...

☆ *Roll of Thunder, Hear My Cry*
Page 87

☆ *The Story of Windrush*
Page 69

HOODOO

BY RONALD L. SMITH

Hoodoo Thatcher's whole family has magic.
Except him.

You'd think because it's his name he'd have even just a little bit of hoodoo, but nope! Hoodoo can barely get a spell out. When a creepy stranger arrives in town, he starts showing up everywhere—even in Hoodoo's dreams. The Stranger makes it clear that he won't let Hoodoo—or anyone else for that matter—get in his way. It's up to Hoodoo and his family to figure out a way to get his magic moving so that he can save everyone—including himself—in their little Alabama town.

QUICK LOOK

This book is about...

☆ Magic
☆ Creepy mysteries

If you like this, check out...

☆ *Just South of Home*
Page 97
☆ *Spirit Hunters*
Page 96

AUTHOR INTERVIEW

What inspired you to write this book?

I wanted to see a young Black boy as a hero—something I didn't see when I was a kid. I also wanted to explore the south and all its customs and flora and fauna.

How did you create the main character in this book?

He just popped into my head one day and demanded that I tell his story. Really.

Where did you write this book? At home? A coffee shop? The library?

All of the above.

What tips do you have for young writers?

Finish your work. Find other writers you like, and share your stories for feedback.

What was the process like in getting this book published?

One of the best experiences of my life. After several failed attempts, I had finally written a book that someone noticed and thought could become a real book!

How do you keep going when you get stuck/writing gets hard?

Listen to music. Take a walk. Eat some potato chips. Also, jump to a new chapter or write the ending.

ABOUT THE AUTHOR

Ronald L. Smith has lived in various places, including Alabama, Washington, D.C., and Japan, but he now lives in Baltimore and writes full time.

What was your favorite middle-grade book as a kid?

Definitely *The Lord of the Rings*. I know it's not a middle-grade book, but I read it during those years. I also loved books by Ray Bradbury and a series called *The Wonderful Flight to the Mushroom Planet*.

What's your favorite word?

Amidst.

HEALER OF THE WATER MONSTER

BY BRIAN YOUNG

Nathan never expected to add saving a Navajo Holy Being to his summer plans. But when he gets lost in the desert near his grandmother Nali's house, that's exactly what he ends up doing.

With his dad focused on a new relationship and his mom focused on her job, Nathan's more than happy to spend his summer away from them in New Mexico. But when Nathan meets a sick water monster whose illness has brought a 30-year drought to Nali's reservation, he must travel to the realm of the Holy Beings. There, he meets more faces from Navajo stories as he tries his hardest to heal the water monster. Along the way, Nathan also searches for healing for his uncle—who suffers from PTSD—and discovers more about his Native heritage and culture.

QUICK LOOK

This book is about...

☆ Adventures in other dimensions

☆ Indigenous culture

If you like this, check out...

☆ *Indian No More*
   Page 60

☆ *The Serpent's Secret*
   Pages 112-113

THE PRINCESS IN BLACK

BY SHANNON & DEAN HALE

Princess Magnolia is almost too perfect in her frilly gown and glittery tiara, so the Duchess suspects the young princess has a secret. And she's right!

In an exciting twist for fairy tale fans, the young princess is also the monster-fighting Princess in Black. She swaps out her pink frills for an all-black mask and cape, but she keeps the tiara (for princess-related reasons). Although the Duchess and the princess's close friend never guess who she is, the Princess in Black always saves the day, battling the many hungry monsters scaring people around the countryside. Be ready for lots of adventure with this not-your-average princess.

QUICK LOOK

This book is about...

☆ Alternative fairy tales
☆ Secret identity

If you like this, check out...

☆ *Jasmine Toguchi, Mochi Queen*   Page 9
☆ *Zombierella: Fairy Tales Gone Bad*   Page 98

THE SAMOSA REBELLION

BY SHANTHI SEKARAN

Muki Krishnan is facing a big problem on the small island of Mariposa.

President Bamberger of Mariposa has declared that there are two groups of people on the island: The "butterflies" are those who've lived on Mariposa for more than three generations. The "moths" are the recent immigrants who are becoming a burden on the "butterflies." His solution? The "moths" must go. When Muki's grandmother is detained in a new camp created to hold "moths" who are going to be deported, Muki joins forces with other revolutionaries. Together, they decide to fight back against the president and his spies in order to overthrow the unjust social and political order threatening their island.

QUICK LOOK

This book is about...

☆ Activism
☆ Immigration

If you like this, check out...

☆ *Efrén Divided*
Page 57
☆ *The Jumbies*
Page 102

RACE TO THE FROZEN NORTH: THE MATTHEW HENSON STORY

BY CATHERINE JOHNSON

Matthew Henson was the first Black man to reach the North Pole. Discover how he got his start on that incredible journey!

As a young boy, Matthew escaped an abusive household and ran away to Washington, D.C., where he worked in a café for food and board. It was there that he realized that the world was bigger than just the little part he'd seen. Matthew began working on ships, learning everything from languages to cooking and carpentry. His talents were eventually recognized, and he became part of an expedition that would become one of the most important discovery missions of all time. Discrimination prevented Matthew from being as celebrated as his white teammates, but this book makes it clear that Matthew Henson is a hero!

QUICK LOOK

This book is about...

☆ Black history

☆ Real-life events

If you like this, check out...

☆ *Sixteen Years in Sixteen Seconds: The Sammy Lee Story*   Page 117

☆ *The Story of Windrush*   Page 69

THE SERPENT'S SECRET

BY SAYANTANI DASGUPTA

On Kiranmala's 12th birthday, there's good news and there's bad news.

The good news is that she's an Indian princess from a different world! The bad news is that her parents have been spirited away, and now she must travel from New Jersey to The Kingdom Beyond to save them. With the help of two princes, a bird, and a magic map, Kiran sets out on a mission to rescue her parents. She must slay demons and deal with snakes—lots of snakes!—to discover the truth about who she really is and decide who she wants to be, despite the role she's been born into.

QUICK LOOK

This book is about...

☆ Adventures in other dimensions
☆ Indian folklore

If you like this, check out...

☆ *Lily & Kosmo in Outer Outer Space*   Page 33
☆ *Sisters of the Neversea* Page 45

AUTHOR INTERVIEW

What inspired you to write this book?

When I was young, I never got to see protagonists who looked like me in books or movies I was exposed to. As an Indian immigrant's daughter, that gave me the message that someone like me didn't deserve to be a hero. Years later, when my own kids were still not seeing themselves in the books they loved, I decided enough was enough. Everyone deserves to see themselves as a hero! So I reached back to my grandmother's Bengali folktales and mixed in some string theory, and *The Kiranmala and the Kingdom Beyond* series was born.

How did you create the main character in this book?

Kiranmala is inspired by an actual heroine from a Bengali folktale. In the original story, she's the younger sister of two brothers, Arun and Barun, who go off on adventures and leave her at home. They underestimate her because she's the girl, but when they get in trouble, it's of course Kiranmala who has to go save them. I loved this idea of the underestimated heroine, so I took that original Kiranmala, put her in a kurta and combat boots, and made her an only child growing up in New Jersey. My modern Kiranmala thinks all the stories her immigrant parents tell her are just dreams and nonsense. But her parents' stories turn out to be true, and she ends up being an intergalactic princess demon slayer!

How do you keep going when you get stuck/writing gets hard?

Every writer gets stuck sometimes. If you're writing on a computer, maybe switch it up and write by hand. I'll sometimes set a timer, tell myself I only have to write for five minutes—a time that doesn't feel too scary—and those short bursts will usually "unstick" me!

ABOUT THE AUTHOR

Sayantani DasGupta grew up in Ohio but spent summer vacations with her family in India. There, she loved when her grandmother would tell her folk tales. She now lives in New York with her family and their black labrador, Khushi, who is scared of almost everything.

What was your favorite middle-grade book as a kid?

A Ring of Endless Light. I loved all Madeline L'Engle's books, but a story about a girl who can talk to dolphins? I was all in.

What's your favorite word?

Gadzooks. But with an exclamation point. Gadzooks!

MALALA: MY STORY OF STANDING UP FOR GIRLS' RIGHTS

BY MALALA YOUSAFZAI & PATRICIA MCCORMICK

Fifteen-year-old Malala Yousafzai's life changed forever in a day—the day she was shot.

Malala lived happily with her friends and family in Mingora, Pakistan. Her father was a school principal and activist who spoke out against the Taliban, and by the time she was a teenager, Malala was following in his footsteps. When she spoke to encourage other girls to stay in school, her voice was heard. That mighty voice was soon to be heard all over the world. The Taliban thought they could silence Malala with a gun, but their efforts only brought her to a bigger stage. Discover Malala's journey as she recovers from life-threatening injuries to become the youngest person ever to win a Noble Peace Prize. An inspiring account of one girl's fight for equality in her own words.

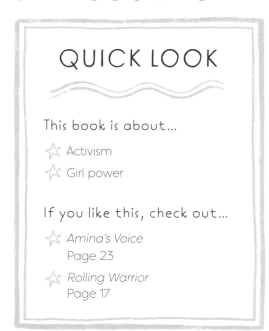

QUICK LOOK

This book is about...
- ☆ Activism
- ☆ Girl power

If you like this, check out...
- ☆ *Amina's Voice*
  Page 23
- ☆ *Rolling Warrior*
  Page 17

OSNAT AND HER DOVE: THE TRUE STORY OF THE WORLD'S FIRST FEMALE RABBI

BY SIGAL SAMUEL

Osnat Barzani lives in 16th-century Mosul, Iraq. Determined and bright, the young Jewish girl persuades her father to teach her to read and write Hebrew.

In Mosul, girls are expected to stick to domestic duties. You don't need to read to do chores! But Osnat has her own ambitions, and she carries on studying. As she grows older, Osnat begins a special friendship with a dove. It keeps her company through all her life changes, including when she steps up to lead her family's yeshiva at a time when it is unheard of for women to teach. After a miraculous incident, people begin to take notice of Osnat. Word of her healing power and wisdom spreads. This is the inspirational true story of a great leader and the first-ever female rabbi.

QUICK LOOK

This book is about...

☆ Girl power
☆ Jewish history

If you like this, check out...

☆ *All Thirteen*
    Pages 118-119

☆ *Amal Unbound*
    Pages 64-65

115

THE BOY WHO HARNESSED THE WIND
BY WILLIAM KAMKWAMBA & BRYAN MEALER

When William Kamkwamba's family loses all their crops to drought, he decides to find a way to care for them.

William can no longer afford to attend school and drops out, but he remains curious and committed to learning. After poring over all the science books in the local library, William decides to build a windmill and radio station with scraps from a junkyard. His thirst for knowledge and willingness to learn leads him to get a different type of education, as he helps his family and his community to survive and thrive.

QUICK LOOK

This book is about...

☆ Black history
☆ Real-life events

If you like this, check out...

☆ *A Single Shard*
   Pages 36–37

☆ *Unspeakable: The Tulsa Race Massacre*   Page 63

SIXTEEN YEARS IN SIXTEEN SECONDS: THE SAMMY LEE STORY

BY PAULA YOO

All Sammy Lee wanted since he was a little boy was to become an Olympic diver.

While he trained for this dream as a child, as a young adult he followed another dream that he shared with his parents: He became a doctor. Then, at 28 years old, Sammy also became the first Asian American to win a gold medal at the Olympic games. After a lifetime of fighting against discrimination, Sammy made his dreams come true and opened the door for many Olympians to dream as big as he did. An inspirational true story of a Korean American child who overcame prejudice to become a national hero.

QUICK LOOK

This book is about...

☆ Racism
☆ Real-life events

If you like this, check out...

☆ *Race to the Frozen North*   Page 111
☆ *The Boy Who Harnessed the Wind*   Page 116

ALL THIRTEEN: THE INCREDIBLE CAVE RESCUE OF THE THAI BOYS' SOCCER TEAM

BY CHRISTINA SOONTORNVAT

When 12 players from the Wild Boars soccer team in Thailand travel to the Nang Non mountains to explore underground caves with their coach, they have no idea that it will be 17 days before they come back out of those caves.

While they're in the caves, a huge storm hits, and when the boys try to leave the tunnels, they find themselves trapped by floodwaters. A team of expert divers, scientists, and rescuers are called in to try to save the team before it's too late. This book tells the incredible story of the people working as part of the rescue mission and how the soccer team themselves relied on their faith and teamwork to stay both calm and hopeful.

QUICK LOOK

This book is about...

⭐ Incredible bravery

⭐ Real-life events

If you like this, check out...

⭐ *Amina's Voice*
Page 23

⭐ *Race to the Frozen North*   Page 111

AUTHOR INTERVIEW

What inspired you to write this book?

I was in Thailand visiting family when the cave rescue took place, and so I knew how emotional and impactful the story was. Once the boys and their coach were all rescued safely, I knew I wanted to write a book about this inspiring event and include as much about Thai culture and community as possible. It really did have such an impact on the mission.

Where did you write this book? At home? A coffee shop? The library?

I was on such a tight deadline for this book, and so I worked on it *everywhere*. My house, the school carpool line, on an airplane, on a train, in a doctor's office waiting room—any chance I got, I was writing!

What tips do you have for young writers?

Don't worry too much about how good your writing is right now. It will get better with practice. Right now, your job is to gather stories and ideas. Talk to people and listen to their stories. Elders—like our grandparents— are particularly great sources. Watch and observe the world around you. Absorb all of these things. Better yet—keep a journal, because you will return to them again and again for inspiration all your life.

How do you keep going when you get stuck/writing gets hard?

Taking a walk outside and getting my blood pumping helps more than anything. I also like to listen to music or watch movies as a way to bust away the clogs in my brain. Sometimes I just need a jolt of some other kind of art to help get me unstuck.

ABOUT THE AUTHOR

Christina Soontornvat grew up in a small town in Texas. Her parents owned a Thai restaurant when she was a kid, and she spent many hours sitting behind the counter reading books. She now lives in Austin, Texas, with her husband, two daughters, and their old cat.

What was your favorite middle-grade book as a kid?

Anything magical, but especially *The Hobbit* by J.R.R. Tolkein.

EL DEAFO

BY CECE BELL

When Cece was little, she got terribly sick. It led to her needing a Phonic Ear hearing aid but also the birth of her superhero alter ego—El Deafo!

Every superhero has a superpower. Cece's is her Phonic Ear that lets her into little secrets others don't know she can hear. But it takes time for Cece to learn how special she is. Feeling different isn't always a good feeling. At a young age, Cece has to change the ways she interacts with the world because of her hearing aid. A new school full of kids and grown-ups who aren't always sensitive to her differences forces Cece to adjust again. In time, Cece realizes that anyone who makes her feel small may not be the best friend to have. Fun, funny, and illustrated with bunnies, this superpowered graphic memoir covers all the fundamental parts of growing up.

QUICK LOOK

This book is about...

☆ Disability

☆ Magical adventures

If you like this, check out...

☆ *New Kid*
  Page 56

☆ *Show Me a Sign*
  Page 59

BIBLIOGRAPHY

Aida Salazar, *The Moon Within* (Scholastic, 2019)

Aisha Saaed, *Amal Unbound* (Penguin Young Readers, 2018)

Alex Gino, *Melissa* (previously published as *George*) (Scholastic, 2022)

Annabelle Sami & Daniela Sosa (Illustrator), *Agent Zaiba Investigates: The Missing Diamonds* (Stripes Publishing, 2020)

Ann Clare LeZotte, *Show Me a Sign* (Scholastic, 2020)

B.B. Alston, *Amari and the Night Brothers* (HarperCollins, 2021)

Ben Hatke, *Little Robot* (First Second, 2015)

Benjamin Dean & Sandhya Prabhat (Illustrator), *Me, My Dad and the End of the Rainbow* (Simon & Schuster, 2021)

Brian Young, *Healer of the Water Monster* (HarperCollins, 2021)

Burhana Islam & Farah Khandaker (Illustrator), *My Laugh-Out-Loud-Life: Mayhem Mission* (Knights Of, 2021)

Carlos Hernandez, *Sal & Gabi Break the Universe* (Disney Press, 2019)

Carole Boston Weatherford & Floyd Cooper (Illustrator), *Unspeakable: The Tulsa Race Massacre* (Lerner Publishing Group, 2021)

Catherine Johnson, *Race to the Frozen North: The Matthew Henson Story* (Barrington Stoke, 2018)

Cece Bell, *El Deafo* (ABRAMS, 2014)

Celia C. Pérez, *The First Rule of Punk* (Penguin Young Readers, 2017)

Charlene Willing McManis & Traci Sorell, *Indian No More* (Lee & Low Books, 2019)

Christina Soontornvat, *All Thirteen: The Incredible Cave Rescue of the Thai Boys' Soccer Team* (Candlewick Press, 2020)

Claribel A. Ortega, *Ghost Squad* (Scholastic, 2020)

Cynthia Leitich Smith, *Sisters of the Neversea* (HarperCollins, 2021)

Dawn Quigley & Tara Audibert (Illustrator), *Jo Jo Makoons: The Used-To-Be Best Friend* (HarperCollins, 2021)

Debbi Michiko Florence & Elizabet Vukovic (Illustrator), *Jasmine Toguchi, Mochi Queen* (Farrar, Straus, and Giroux 2017)

Debbie Levy, *The Year of Goodbyes* (Little, Brown, 2019)

Elle McNicoll, *A Kind of Spark* (Random House Children's, 2021)

Ellen Oh, *Spirit Hunters* (HarperCollins, 2017)

Erica Armstrong Dunbar, *Never Caught, the Story of Ona Judge* (Young Reader's Edition) Aladdin, 2019)

Ernesto Cisneros, *Efrén Divided* (HarperCollins, 2020)

E.L. Konigsburg, *From the Mixed-Up Files of Mrs. Basil E. Frankweiler* (Atheneum Books for Young Readers, 1998)

Erin Entrada Kelly, *Hello, Universe* (HarperCollins, 2017)

Gene Luen Yang, *Prime Baby* (First Second, 2010)

Hena Khan, *Amina's Voice* (Salaam Reads/Simon & Schuster, 2017)

Jacqueline Woodson, *Brown Girl Dreaming* (Penguin Young Readers, 2014)

Jasmine Warga, *Other Words for Home* (HarperCollins, 2019)

Jason Reynolds & Selom Sunu (Illustrator), *Look Both Ways: A Tale Told in Ten Blocks* (Atheneum/Caitlyn Dlouhy Books, 2019)

Jerry Craft, *New Kid* (HarperCollins, 2019)

Jessica Kim, *Stand Up, Yumi Chung!* (Penguin Young Readers, 2020)

Jessie Janowitz, *The Doughnut Fix* (Sourcebooks Inc., 2018)

Jonathan Ashley, *Lily & Kosmo in Outer Outer Space* (Simon & Schuster, 2018)

Joseph Coelho & Freya Hartas (Illustrator), *Zombierella: Fairy Tales Gone Bad* (Walker Books, 2020)

Judith Heumann & Kristen Joiner, *Rolling Warrior* (Beacon Press, 2021)

Julie Murphy, *Dear Sweet Pea* (HarperCollins, 2019)

Kacen Callender, *Hurricane Child* (Scholastic, 2018)

Karen Strong, *Just South of Home* (Simon & Schuster, 2019)

Katherine Arden, *Small Spaces* (Penguin Young Readers, 2018)

Katherine Marsh, *Nowhere Boy* (Roaring Brook Press, 2018)

Katie Tsang, Kevin Tsang, & Nathan Reed (Illustrator), *Sam Wu is NOTAfraid of Ghosts* (Union Square Kids, 2018)

Kekla Magoon, *The Season of Styx Malone* (Random House Children's, 2018)

Kelly Starling Lyons & Vanessa Brantley-Newton (Illustrator), *Jada Jones: Rock Star* (Penguin Young Readers, 2017)

Kelly Yang & Maike Plenzke (Illustrator), *Front Desk* (Scholastic, 2018)

K.N. Chimbiri, *The Story of the Windrush* (Scholastic, 2020)

Kwame Alexander, Chris Colderley, and Marjory Wentworth & Ekua Holmes (Illustrator),
Out of Wonder (Candlewick Press, 2017)

Lamar Giles & Dapo Adeola (Illustrator), *The Last Last-Day-of-Summer* (HarperCollins, 2019)

Leah Henderson, *The Magic in Changing Your Stars* (Union Square Kids, 2020)

Linda Sue Park, *A Single Shard* (HarperCollins, 2001)

Lisa Fipps, *Starfish* (Penguin Young Readers, 2021)

Lisa Moore Ramée, *A Good Kind of Trouble* (HarperCollins, 2019)

Louis Sachar, *Holes* (Random House Children's, 1999)

Maisie Chan & Anh Cao (Illustrator), *Danny Chung Does Not Do Maths* (Piccadilly Press, 2021)

Malala Yousafzai & Patricia McCormick, *Malala: My Story of Standing Up for Girls' Rights* (Little, Brown, 2018)

Mark Oshiro, *The Insiders* (HarperCollins, 2021)

Marti Dumas & Stephanie Parcus (Illustrator), *Jupiter Storm* (Yes, MAM Creations, 2017)

Meg Medina, *Merci Suárez Changes Gears* (Candlewick Press, 2018)

Mildred D. Taylor, *Roll of Thunder, Hear My Cry* (Penguin Young Readers, 2001)

Monica Brown & Angela N. Dominguez (Illustrator), *Lola Levine Is Not Mean!* (Little, Brown, 2016)

Neil Gaiman & Chris Riddell (Illustrator), *The Graveyard Book* (HarperCollins, 2008)

Nic Stone, *Fast Pitch* (Random House Children's, 2021)

Nikki Grimes & R. Gregory Christie (Illustrator), *Make Way for Dyamonde Daniel* (Penguin Young Readers, 2009)

Nikole Hannah-Jones, Renée Watson, & Nikkolas Smith (Illustrator),
The 1619 Project: Born on the Water (Penguin Young Readers, 2021)

Olugbemisola Rhuday-Perkovich, *Two Naomis* (HarperCollins, 2016)

Parinita Shetty, *The A-Z Djinn Detective Agency* (Penguin Random House, 2016)

Paula Chase, *So Done* (HarperCollins, 2018)

Paula Danziger & Tony Ross (Illustrator), *Amber Brown Is Not a Crayon* (Penguin Young Readers, 2006)

Paula Yoo & Dom Lee (Illustrator), *Sixteen Years in Sixteen Seconds: The Sammy Lee Story* (Lee & Low Books, 2010)

Rebecca K.S. Ansari, *The Missing Piece of Charlie O'Reilly* (HarperCollins, 2019)

Remy Lai, *Pie In the Sky* (Henry Holt & Co., 2019)

Renée Watson & Nina Mata (Illustrator), *Ways to Make Sunshine* (Bloomsbury, 2020)

Rex Ogle, *Free Lunch* (Norton Young Readers, 2019)

Rita Williams-Garcia, *One Crazy Summer* (HarperCollins, 2010)

Rob Harrell, *Wink* (Penguin Young Readers, 2020)

Ronald L. Smith, *Hoodoo* (HarperCollins, 2017)

Samantha Baines & Jessica Flores (Illustrator), *Harriet Versus the Galaxy* (Knights Of, 2019)

Sayantani DasGupta, *The Serpent's Secret* (Scholastic, 2018)

Serena Patel & Emma McCann (Illustrator), *Anisha, Accidental Detective* (Usborne, 2020)

Shannon Hale, Dean Hale, & LeUyen Pham (Illustrator), *The Princess in Black* (Candlewick Press, 2014)

Shanthi Sekaran, *The Samosa Rebellion* (HarperCollins, 2021)

Sharon M. Draper, *Blended* (Atheneum/Caitlyn Dlouhy Books, 2018)

Sharna Jackson, *High-Rise Mystery* (Knights Of, 2019)

Sigal Samuel & Vali Mintzi (Illustrator), *Osnat and Her Dove: The True Story
of the World's First Female Rabbi* (Levine Querido, 2021)

Supriya Kelkar, *American as Paneer Pie* (Simon & Schuster, 2020)

Susan Tan & Dana Wulfekotte (Illustrator), *Cilla Lee-Jenkins: Future Author Extraordinaire* (Square Fish, 2018)

Tehlor Kay Mejia, *Paola Santiago and the River of Tears* (Disney Press, 2020)

Thanhha Lai, *Inside Out & Back Again* (HarperCollins, 2011)

Tonya Bolden, *Maritcha: A Nineteenth-Century American Girl* (Abrams Books for Young Readers, 2005)

Tracey Baptiste, *The Jumbies* (Algonquin Young Readers, 2015)

Veera Hiranandani, *The Night Diary* (Penguin Young Readers, 2018)

Victoria Schwab, *City of Ghosts* (Scholastic, 2018)

Virginia Hamilton, *The House of Dies Drear* (Aladdin, 2006)

William Kamkwamba & Bryan Mealer, *The Boy Who Harnessed the Wind* (Penguin Young Readers, 2016)

Zanib Mian & Nasaya Mafaridik (Illustrator), *Planet Omar: Accidental Trouble Magnet* (Penguin Young Readers, 2020)

Zetta Elliott & Geneva B (Illustrator), *Dragons in a Bag* (Random House Children's, 2018)

CONVERSATION STARTERS

Do you like to read books? Why/why not?

What is your favorite book and why?

Who is your favorite character from a book and why?

Do you see yourself in the books you read and the characters in them?
Why/why not?

Why do you think it is important for everyone to see
themselves represented in books?

Which books from this collection would you like to read?

Which authors from this collection would you like to look out
for in your local library or bookstore?

Which books or poems in this collection include events that
have happened to you?

Which books or poems in this collection have characters that you recognize?

Which books or poems in this collection include events
that haven't happened to you?

Which books or poems in this collection have characters that
are different from you in some way?

How did seeing characters and events that you have
experienced make you feel?

How did seeing characters and events that you haven't
experienced make you feel?

WRITING YOUR OWN STORIES

Have the author interviews in this book inspired you to write your own story or poetry? If so, here are some things you might want to think about...

BACKSTORY

These are the things that happened to the characters before the first page of the book. Backstories help us to understand why characters do things and how they see the world.

> **Prompt**

Think about the things that have happened to you up until today—what is your backstory? What backstories do you think make interesting characters?

CONFLICT

All stories have conflict, and it is the main issue that the characters must solve.

> **Prompt**

Think about your favorite book, or one of the books in this collection—what was the conflict? Who was it between?

CHARACTERIZATION

This is the way you describe a character. A character can be described in just one word—such as "friendly" or "mean"—but the things they do can also describe them. For example, if a character steals a bike, we know that they are a thief.

> **Prompt**

Think about the characters of your story. Make a list of simple words to describe them. Now make another list of things that they do that shows their character.

E.g., "Helpful" Jason carries his elderly neighbor's shopping in from the car.

"Friendly" Jason waves at the mailman and flashes him a big smile.

DIALOGUE

These are the words spoken by the characters in a book. The dialogue is how we understand more about what the characters think and how they feel. It can also help move the plot along.

> **Prompt**

Think about the dialogue in books that you've read. Is the dialogue of every character the same, or is it different? What does the dialogue tell us about the character? Try writing dialogue for the characters in your story.

IMAGERY

We can use words and language to add to the mood of a setting or incident. Think about how different types of imagery are used in different types of stories. In spooky stories, for example, the imagery is often dark and stormy, which helps us understand that something strange is about to happen. In stories set by the beach in summer, the imagery is bright and bold, and so we know that this is a happy setting.

> **Prompt**

How has imagery been used in stories that you've read? What sort of story would you like to write, and how could imagery help bring that story to life for the reader?

PLOT

These are the events of the story. Usually the plot revolves around the conflict and how to resolve it.

> **Prompt**

What is the plot of your favorite story? What would be the plot of your story?

PROTAGONIST

This is the main character in the story. They are usually the person who you want to come out on top in the end.

> **Prompt**

What kind of protagonists do you like to read about? Super brave and loud protagonists, or ones who are shy and quiet? What would the protagonist of your story be like?

SETTING

This is where and when the story is taking place. You can pick any time and place for a story—it can be set hundreds of years in the past, or thousands of years in the future, and the place doesn't even have to be real!

> **Prompt**

What is the setting of your favorite book? What do you think would make an interesting setting for a story? How does the setting affect other things, like the plot and the dialogue?

INDEX

1619 Project: Born on the Water, The 68

A

activism 17, 62, 66, 110, 114
Agent Zaiba Investigates: The Missing Diamonds 78
Alexander, Kwame 24
aliens 47, 52
All Thirteen: The Incredible Cave Rescue of the Thai Boys' Soccer Team 118–119
Alston, B. B. 73
Amal Unbound 64–65
Amari and the Night Brothers 73
Amber Brown Is Not a Crayon 8
American as Paneer Pie 22
Amina's Voice 23
Anisha, Accidental Detective 77
Arden, Katherine 103
Ashley, Jonathan 33
A Single Shard 36–37
autism 28
A-Z Djinn Detective Agency 76

B

Baines, Samantha 47
baking 50–51, 74
Baptiste, Tracey 102
Black experience 56, 62, 75, 84
Black history 16, 41, 63, 66, 68, 69, 97, 105, 111, 116
Blended 25
Bolden, Tonya 66
Boy Who Harnessed the Wind, The 116
Brown Girl Dreaming 84
Brown, Monica 11
bullying 11, 39, 40, 54, 56, 88, 90

C

Callender, Kacen 90
Caribbean folklore 102
Chan, Maisie 86
Chase, Paula 94
Chimbiri, K. N. 69
Chinese culture 13, 54, 86
Cilla Lee-Jenkins: Future Author Extraordinaire 13
Cisneros, Ernesto 57
City of Ghosts 100–101
Coelho, Joseph 98
courage 23, 54, 118–119
Craft, Jerry 56

D

Danny Chung Does Not Do Maths 86
Danziger, Paula 8
Dean, Benjamin 91
DasGupta, Sayantani 112–113
Dear Sweet Pea 39
disability 17, 58, 120
displacement 40, 60, 61, 70. 81
Doughnut Fix, The 55
Dragons in a Bag 35
Draper, Sharon M. 25
Dumas, Marti 15
Dunbar, Erica Armstrong 41

E

Efrén Divided 57
Elliott, Zetta 35

F

fairy tales, alternative 98, 109
families 13, 14, 16, 18–19, 32, 54, 61, 74, 79, 84, 85, 86, 87, 96, 97, 102
   blended 25, 45
   changing 8, 25, 82–83, 91
   loss of family members 38, 40, 50–51, 95, 103
   secrets 15, 47
   separated 57
   spirits of 99
   weddings 48, 77
Fast Pitch 85
Fipps, Lisa 21
First Rule of Punk, The 29
fitting in 10, 18–19, 44, 88–89
Free Lunch 67
friendships 35, 39, 80, 82–83, 88–89, 92–93, 100–101, 104
   changing 6–7, 8, 94
   new 10, 12, 26–27, 38, 44, 55, 67, 70, 90
From the Desk of Zoe Washington 74
From the Mixed-Up Files of Mrs. Basil E. Frankweiler 72
Front Desk 34

G

Gaiman, Neil 95
ghosts 54, 96, 99, 100–101
Ghost Squad 99
Giles, Lamar 53
Gino, Alex 30–31
girl power 11, 32, 64–65, 78, 98, 114, 115
Good Kind of Trouble, A 62
Graveyard Book, The 95
Grimes, Nikki 12
growing pains 11, 14, 20, 39, 56, 92–93, 94

H

Hale, Shannon 109
Hamilton, Virginia 105
Hannah-Jones, Nikole 68
Harrell, Rob 58
Harriet Versus the Galaxy 47
Hatke, Ben 44
haunted places 96, 97, 105
Healer of the Water Monster 108
Hello, Universe 88–89
Henderson, Leah 32
Hernandez, Carlos 38
Heumann, Judith 17
High-Rise Mystery 75
Hindu culture 77
Hiranandani, Veera 61
historical events 28, 59, 61, 63, 66, 81
Holes 71
Hoodoo 106–107
House of Dies Drear, The 105
Hurricane Child 90

I

immigrants 34, 40, 42–43, 50–51, 57, 69, 110
Indian culture 22, 48, 76
Indian folklore 112–113
Indian No More 60
Indigenous culture 6–7, 60, 108
Inside Out & Back Again 40
Insiders, The 26–27
intergalactic adventures 47, 52, 73
Islam, Burhana 48

J

Jackson, Sharna 75
Jada Jones: Rock Star 10
Janowitz, Jessie 55
Japanese culture 9
Jasmine Toguchi, Mochi Queen 9
Jewish history 81, 115
Johnson, Catherine 111
Joiner, Kristen 17
Jo Jo Makoons: The Used-To-Be Best Friend 6–7
Jumbies, The 102
Jupiter Storm 15
Just South of Home 97

K

Kamkwamba, William 116
Kelkar, Supriya 22
Kelly, Erin Entrada 88–89
Khan, Hena 23
Kim, Jessica 49

Kind of Spark, A 28
Konigsburg, E. L. 72
Korean culture 36–37

L

Lai, Remy 50–51
Lai, Thanhha 40
Last Last-Day-Of-Summer, The 53
Latinx folklore 104
Levy, Debbie 81
LeZotte, Ann Clare 59
LGBTQ+ 20, 26–27, 30–31, 90, 91
Lily & Kosmo in Outer Outer Space 33
Little Robot 44
Lola Levine Is Not Mean! 11
Look Both Ways: A Tale Told in Ten Blocks 92–93
Lyons, Kelly Starling 10

M

magic 15, 26–27, 32, 45, 53, 76, 79, 106–107, 120
Magic in Changing Your Stars, The 32
Magoon, Kekla 80
Make Way for Dyamonde Daniel 12
Malala: My Story of Standing Up for Girls' Rights 114
Maritcha: A Nineteenth-Century American Girl 66
Marks, Janae 74
Marsh, Katherine 70
McCormick, Patricia 114
McManus, Charlene Willing 60
McNicoll, Elle 28
Mealer, Bryan 116
Medina, Meg 18–19
Mejia, Tehlor Kay 104
Melissa (George) 30–31
Me, My Dad and the End of the Rainbow 91
Merci Suárez Changes Gears 18–19
Mian, Zanib 46
Michiko Florence, Debbi 9
Missing Piece of Charlie O'Reilly, The 79
Moon Within, The 20
moving home 8, 12, 14, 26, 29, 46, 55, 84, 96
Murphy, Julie 39
music and dance 20, 23, 29, 32, 94
Muslim culture 42, 46
My Laugh-Out-Loud Life: Mayhem Mission 48
mysteries 53, 72, 85, 106

N

Never Caught, The Story of Ona Judge 41
New Kid 56
Night Diary, The 61
Nowhere Boy 70

O

Ogle, Rex 67
Oh, Ellen 96
One Crazy Summer 16
Ortega, Claribel A. 99
Oshiro, Mark 26–27
Osnat and Her Dove: The True Story of the World's First Female Rabbi 115
other dimensions 32, 34, 38, 108, 112–113
Other Words for Home 42–43
Out of Wonder 24

P

Pakistani culture 61, 78
Paola Santiago and the River of Tears 104
parents 90, 104
  divorce 8, 25, 39, 82–83, 91
  loss of 38, 40, 50–51, 103
Park, Linda Sue 36¬–37
Patel, Serena 77
Pérez, Celia C. 29
Pie in the Sky 50–51
Planet Omar: Accidental Trouble Magnet 46
poetry 24, 68, 81, 84
Prime Baby 52
Princess in Black, The 109

Q, R

Quigley, Dawn 6–7
Race to the Frozen North: The Matthew Henson Story 111
racism 23, 25, 34, 40, 59, 62, 63, 74, 87, 97, 117
Ramée, Lisa Moore 62
real-life events 111, 116, 117, 118–119
Reynolds, Jason 92–93
Rhuday-Perkovich, Olugbemisola 82–83
Rolling Warrior 17
Roll of Thunder, Hear My Cry 87

S

Saaed, Aisha 64–65
Sachar, Louis 71
Sal & Gabi Break the Universe 38
Salazar, Aida 20
Sami, Annabelle 78
Samosa Rebellion, The 110
Samuel, Sigal 115
Sam Wu is Not Afraid of Ghosts 54
Schwab, Victoria 100–101
Season of Styx Malone, The 80
secrets 47, 72
  secret identities 109
Sekaran, Shanthi 110
Serpent's Secret, The 112–113
Shetty, Parinita 76
Show Me a Sign 59

siblings 16, 72, 73, 75, 79, 80
  new 13, 52
Sisters of the Neversea 45
Sixteen Years in Sixteen Seconds: The Sammy Lee Story 117
slavery 41, 66, 68
Small Spaces 103
Smith, Cynthia L. 45
Smith, Ronald L. 106–107
So Done 94
Soontornvat, Christina 118–119
Sorell, Traci 60
Spirit Hunters 96
Stand Up, Yumi Chung! 49
Starfish 21
Stone, Nic 85
Story of the Windrush, The 69
Strong, Karen 97

T, U

Tan, Susan 13
Taylor, Mildred D. 87
Tsang, Katie and Kevin 54
Two Naomis 82–83
Unspeakable: The Tulsa Race Massacre 63

W

Warga, Jasmine 42–43
Watson, Renée 14, 68
Weatherford, Carole Boston 63
Ways to Make Sunshine 14
Williams-Garcia, Rita 16
Wink 58
witches 28, 35, 99
Woodson, Jacqueline 84

Y, Z

Yang, Gene Luen 52
Yang, Kelly 34
Year of Goodbyes, The 81
Yoo, Paula 117
Young, Brian 108
Yousafzai, Malala 114
Zombierella: Fairy Tales Gone Bad 98

Editor Vicky Armstrong
Senior Designer Nathan Martin
Designer Maisy Ruffels
Production Editor Siu Yin Chan
Senior Production Controller Louise Minihane
Senior Acquisitions Editor Katy Flint
Managing Art Editor Vicky Short
Publishing Director Mark Searle

ACKNOWLEDGEMENTS
DK would like to thank the team at We Need Diverse Books;
all of the sensitivity readers; Julia March for the index;
and Jennette ElNaggar for proofreading.

Published by Dorling Kindersley Ltd in association with We Need Diverse Books

First American Edition, 2022
Published in the United States by DK Publishing
1745 Broadway, 20th Floor, New York, NY 10019

Foreword copyright © Ellen Oh, 2022
Artwork copyright © Katherine Ahmed, Jake Alexander, Tequitia Andrews,
Ruth Burrows, and Janeen Constantino, 2022

PICTURE CREDITS
The publisher would like to thank the following for their kind permission to reproduce their photographs:
19 Sonya Sones; 27 Zoraida Córdova; 31 Blake C Aarens;
83 Kikelomo Amusa-Shonubi; 101 Jenna Maurice; 119 Sam Bond Photography

Copyright © 2022 Dorling Kindersley Limited
DK, a Division of Penguin Random House LLC
22 23 24 25 26 10 9 8 7 6 5 4 3 2 1
001-328487-Oct/22

A catalog record for this book is available from the Library of Congress.
ISBN 978-0-7440-5788-1
DK books are available at special discounts when purchased in bulk for sales promotions, premiums,
fund-raising, or educational use. For details, contact: DK Publishing Special Markets, 1745 Broadway, 20th
Floor, New York, NY 10019 Email: SpecialSales@dk.com

Printed and bound in Slovakia
For the curious
www.dk.com

MIX
Paper | Supporting
responsible forestry
FSC™ C018179

This book is made from
Forest Stewardship Council™
certified paper—one small
step in DK's commitment
to a sustainable future.